The Public Trust

and the

First Americans

The Center for the Study of the First Americans

The Center for the Study of the First Americans is an affiliate of the Department of Anthropology at Oregon State University, established in July 1981 by a seed grant from Mr. William Bingham's Trust for Charity. Its goals are to encourage research about Pleistocene peoples of the Americas, and to make this new knowledge available to both the scientific community and the interested public. Toward this end, the Center staff is developing research, public outreach, and publications programs.

The Center's Peopling of the Americas publication program focuses on the earliest Americans and their environments. The Center also publishes a quarterly newspaper called the *Mammoth Trumpet*, written for both a general and a professional audience, as well as an annual journal, *Current Research in the Pleistocene*, which presents note-length articles about current research in the interdisciplinary field of Quaternary studies as they relate to the Pleistocene peopling of the Americas.

Manuscript Submissions
BOOKS
The Center solicits high-quality original manuscripts in English. For information write to: Robson Bonnichsen, Center for the Study of the First Americans, Department of Anthropology, Oregon State University, Corvallis, OR 97331 or call (503) 737-4596.

CURRENT RESEARCH IN THE PLEISTOCENE
Researchers wishing to submit summaries in this annual serial should contact editor Bradley T. Lepper, Ohio High School, 1982 Velma Avenue, Columbus, OH 43211-2497 or request Information for Contributors from the Center. The deadline for submission is January 31 of each calendar year; early submission is suggested.

MAMMOTH TRUMPET
News of discoveries, reports on recent conferences, book reviews, and news of current issues invited. Contact editor Don Hall, Center for the Study of the First Americans at (503) 745-5203.

ADDITIONALLY . . .
Authors are encouraged to submit reprints of published articles or copies of unpublished papers for inclusion in the Center's research library. Exchanges of relevant books and periodicals with other publishers is also encouraged. Please address contributions and correspondence to the Center's library.

The Public Trust

and the

First Americans

Ruthann Knudson

Bennie C. Keel

Editors

Oregon State University Press
for the
The Center for the Study of the First Americans

Corvallis, Oregon

The paper in this book meets the guidelines for permanence and durability of the Committee on Production Guidelines for Book Longevity of the Council on Library Resources and the minimum requirements of the American National Standard for Permanence of Paper for Printed Library Materials Z39.48-1984.

Library of Congress Cataloging-in-Publication Data

The public trust and the First Americans / Ruthann Knudson & Bennie C. Keel, editors.

   p. cm.

Papers presented at the Public Trust Symposium at the World Summit Conference on the Peopling of the Americas, held at the University of Maine, Orono, May 24-28, 1989.

Includes bibliographical references and index.

ISBN 0-87071-025-7 (alk. paper)

1. Indians of North America—Antiquities—Collection and preservation—Congresses. 2. Indians of North America—Antiquities—Law and legislation—Congresses. 3. Archaeology—United States—Moral and ethical aspects—Congresses. 4. Cultural property, Protection of—United States—Congresses. 5. United States—Antiquities—Congresses. I. Knudson, Ruthann. II. Keel, Bennie C., 1934-   . III. Center for the Study of the First Americans (Oregon State University). IV. Public Trust Symposium (1989 : University of Maine)

E77.9.P62 1995

973.1—dc20   95-7423

                                              CIP

To

Hannah Marie Wormington

1914-1994

"In the future, as in the past, the gathering of information will depend to a great extent on cooperation between avocational and professional archaeologists"

—H.M. Wormington
Colorado Archaeological Society, 1978

Foreword

Dennis Stanford

This volume focuses on the concept that the archaeological remains of the First Americans are part of a public trust to be protected and used to the benefit of all people: the general public, avocational archaeologists, Native Americans, and professional archaeologists alike. As with all trust relationships, there are mutual responsibilities. Avocational archaeologists know the land and its resources perhaps better than do most professional archaeologists, who spend most of their time teaching, in museums, or managing public and private organizations. In this foreword, the relationship between the avocational and professional archaeologist is emphasized.

There is currently distrust among amateurs, professional archaeologists, and Native Americans where partnerships are needed to meet public trust responsibilities. Recent U.S. archaeological protection laws have inhibited cooperation among these groups, and efforts need to be made to re-establish connections for inventory, analysis, and interpretation. Partnerships are based on earned respect and mutual expectations. For example, the general public as well as archaeologists need to respect the spiritual qualities of ancient Native American sites and artifacts. And scientific analysis of First Americans' physical remains can provide much needed information important to addressing modern Native American health issues and supporting additional Native American understanding of their past.

Paleoindian studies are multidisciplinary and require a variety of scientific expertise and significant local knowledge. Most Paleoindian sites have been found and reported by avocational archaeologists and interested landowners or by geologists in the course of their research. Once they have been found, it is the responsibility of the professional archaeologist to insure that the archaeological information is carefully recovered, analyzed, synthesized, reported in both technical journals and popular publications, and managed for future generations. It is the responsibility of all to see that the First American sites are protected from development or destruction. Through a partnership in the public trust all groups have an opportunity to participate in the past and help bring the past back to life as an understanding of who we are, where we came from, and why we are the way we are.

Preface

The World Summit Conference on the Peopling of the Americas was held at the University of Maine, Orono, May 24-28, 1989. The conference was sponsored by the Center for the Study of the First Americans, then located within the University's Institute for Quaternary Studies and now an integral part of Oregon State University, Corvallis. Most of the conference consisted of presentations about current research on the earliest people in the Americas, but within the conference the Public Trust Symposium was devoted to understanding the public context in which that research is conducted, and in which First Americans resources are used, preserved, or destroyed. This volume includes the symposium presentations, plus a summary of the conference research presentations (Bonnichsen et al.) and a final overview on the topic of the public trust and the First Americans (Keel and Calabrese).

Acknowledgments

Many people contributed to the Public Trust Symposium from which the papers included in this volume were derived, and to the transition from a set of spoken ideas to a crafted book. Robson Bonnichsen, Director of the Center for the Study of the First Americans (CSFA), organized and chaired the First World Summit Conference, initiated the idea of the Public Trust Symposium and has supported its publication. The editors particularly appreciate his support, and that of other CSFA staff members in Orono (Louise Bennett, Judith Cooper, and John Tomenchuk) and Corvallis (Patti Good, Rebecca Foster) from 1988 until publication of this volume. In complement, the contributions of all symposium participants and volume authors are also acknowledged with appreciation. Papers in this volume by Bense, Devine, Douglas, Fowler, Gallant, Knudson, Le

Master, Magne, McGimsey, Watson, and Williams were presented orally in the symposium. The paper here by McManamon and Knudson is based on an oral symposium presentation of the same name by George S. Smith, Francis P. McManamon, and Richard C. Waldbauer. The papers here by Bonnichsen et al. and by Keel and Calabrese were written specifically for this volume, and are based on other conference discussions and the symposium presentations.

The U.S. National Park Service (NPS) sponsored the Public Trust Symposium and provided travel funds from the U.S. Department of the Interior Office of the Departmental Consulting Archeologist (ODCA; Bennie C. Keel, then DCA), Washington, DC, under a NPS-University of Maine Cooperative Agreement (CA 1600-5-0005) administered by the Scientific Studies Program, NPS North Atlantic Regional Office, Boston. This ODCA support provided travel expenses to the conference for Judith A. Bense, John G. Douglas, Roy Gallant, Leslie Starr Hart, Ruthann Knudson, Dennis C. Le Master, Charles R. McGimsey, III, George S. Smith, Patty Jo Watson, and Steve Williams. The CSFA provided travel support for Heather Devine and Martin P.R. Magne. Expenses of other symposium participants were supported by their home institutions.

Ruthann Knudson's participation prior to April 1990 was a contribution of Knudson Associates, of which she is the principal, except for the previously acknowledged ODCA travel support. Her subsequent involvement in the development of this volume has been a contribution of the ODCA and NPS Archeological Assistance Division (Francis P. McManamon, DCA and Division Chief), and Knudson Associates. Jean Alexander, Ruthann Knudson, and Jo Alexander technically edited the volume. Bennie Keel's involvement in the planning of the symposium and preparation of this volume has also been supported by the NPS, through either the ODCA or the Southeast Archeological Center, Tallahassee. F.A. Calabrese's participation in this volume has been supported by the NPS Midwest Archeological Center, Lincoln. Subvention of this volume's printing costs was provided by the ODCA.

Contents

I. Public Stewardship of First Americans Resources

first, *adj.* 1. being before all others with respect to time . . .
American, *adj.* 5. . . . an inhabitant of the Western Hemisphere.

First Americans are the subject of public fascination and
scholarly research, that research including the development
of models of past human adaptation to changing world
climates and ecosystems. Their archaeological, geological,
and paleoenvironmental remains are nonrenewable—once
gone, they are gone forever. A critical factor in gleaning
information about the First Americans—the people, their
lifeways, and their world—is the interrelationships among
these remains and the contexts in which the information is
found. Nothing is simple about understanding the First
Americans.

This volume was developed out of a symposium on
public responsibilities for protection of First Americans
resources, including discussions of

  • the concept of that responsibility;

  • relationships among researchers working on First
Americans resources that are often publicly managed, and
those resource managers;

  • the legal basis for protecting First Americans resources
in the Americas and related materials in Asia;

  • opportunities for educating the public about the First
Americans and their information values; and

  • how to pay for First Americans research and protection
of resources.

First Americans resources, be they archaeological or noncultural paleoenvironmental sites, collections, or related records, are nonrenewable and finite. The use of these resources must be carefully managed, conserving while at the same time exploiting them to create public information. Around the world, a variety of private and public individuals and organizations manage the use of First Americans materials. The Public Trust Symposium was cosponsored by the National Park Service and the Center for the Study of the First Americans, and focused on the public nature of these resources and the various aspects involved in its wise use—a public ethic of stewardship, the public context in which research is conducted, the legal environment of resource management, and public education about and financial support for research and management. The National Park Service's concerns about First Americans resource stewardship, as expressed by Leslie Starr Hart, reflect the need of most land managers for information about First Americans research and how to protect First Americans resources so that those managers can be better public servants.

Ruthann Knudson
Bennie C. Keel

The First Americans and the National Park Service

Leslie Starr Hart

The National Park Service requests technical guidance regarding the role of indigenous populations in First Americans research, methods for achieving cooperation and information exchange among federal, tribal, state and private sectors in Arctic research, and ways to enhance ongoing and developing international scientific exchanges.

Federal Management Needs

The U.S. National Park Service (NPS)'s cosponsorship of the international multi-disciplinary World Summit Conference on the Peopling of the Americas, specifically of the Public Trust Symposium, is very appropriate. It is obvious that the synthesis of scientific information and the delineation of priorities resulting from these deliberations will assist us not only in managing archaeological resources on our park lands but, perhaps more importantly, in our efforts to provide leadership and coordination for federal, tribal, state, and local agencies in managing, interpreting, and preserving the archaeological resources that are the focus of this meeting.

(1) The involvement of indigenous populations (local residents) in the development and implementation of research in areas that may have direct bearing on their ability to continue a subsistence-based way of life. Many of these people, living in remote areas, represent cultures "on the brink"; however, they possess an evolved competency for survival in a stressed environment that we would do well to consider and learn from.

(2) The ongoing development and implementation of basic and applied research under the Arctic Research and Policy Act of 1984. This Act stresses the coordination of Arctic research, through interagency federal/state and private sector cooperation with respect to planning and data sharing. It could,

and should, include research related to the peopling of the Americas.

(3) The enhancement of ongoing and developing international exchanges among scientists and scholars. Alaska has been the beneficiary of *glasnost* with the former Union of Socialist Soviet Republics in a very positive manner since 1987. We hope to expand these cooperative endeavors into the circumpolar and FennoScandia regions and beyond.

Being associated with the First World Summit Conference provides a certain sense of history. One cannot help but wonder what effect this will have on the global vision of American origins. For truly this is a global question, one that overrides the geopolitical boundaries presently dividing the planet. These boundaries have at times clouded issues relating to human occupation of the Americas, but are overcome by cooperation and exchange of information among those whose research addresses the peopling of the Americas—in Asia, North America, and Central and South America. Although the conference is divided along these traditional lines, I trust that these organizational constructs will provide a common ground, an academic landscape, if you will, on which there can be a fruitful exchange of ideas and a consensus of direction.

As a manager, I am very pleased to see that the conference not only addresses questions concerning current research and data gaps, the establishment of priorities for future research, the legal environment for addressing archaeological resource management, and funding for this research, but also issues related to the protection of the resource as exemplified in conference topics concerning public education, preservation of the public trust, and the stewardship of the archaeological record throughout the Americas. Given the fact that the majority of the archaeology conducted in the Americas is funded by the public, it is clear that the public has a big stake in archaeology. It is also clear that protection of the resource requires the active participation of the public. Increasing the public's awareness of and appreciation for archaeology will no doubt result in increased protection of the archaeological resource base throughout the Americas.

Before we can effectively protect, study, and manage the archaeological resource base, we must determine how big it is and what it consists of. Estimates by federal agencies in the United States indicate that there are approximately 425,000 known archeological sites on federally managed U.S. lands. Take into consideration that these same agencies report that approximately 93 percent of their land has not been examined for archaeological sites and the size of the actual archaeological database will be seen to be tremendously understated. But even this conservative estimate, of course, does not include the state and private lands which make up approximately two-thirds of the United States. If this level of survey is indicative of efforts in other parts of the Americas, and I think it likely is, then we have a long way to go in terms of defining the archaeological resource base. No doubt many of the sites still undiscovered could address questions relating to the peopling of the Americas and our efforts to understand this topic would be enhanced by research designed to locate and inventory these sites.

Inventory Enhancement

Since 1971, U.S. federal agencies have been mandated to inventory their lands for archaeological resources. A 1988 amendment (P.L. 100-555) to the Archaeological Resources Protection Act of 1979 mandates federal agencies to "develop plans for surveying lands under their control to determine the nature and extent of archaeological resources on those lands [and to] prepare a schedule for surveying lands that are likely to contain the most scientifically valuable archaeological resources." Although mandated, no funds have to date been allocated for extensive archaeological inventory (cf. Le Master, this volume). Instead the charge has been to inventory within existing programs and budgets—to do more with less. It is not surprising that less than seven percent of federal lands in the United States have been surveyed for archaeological sites. The archaeological resources of an even smaller percentage of

American lands outside of the United States have been inventoried.

In setting priorities and making recommendations for archaeological inventory in the Americas and other appropriate geographical areas, consideration should be given to cooperative academic-government research efforts, perhaps in the form of joint projects or studies involving scientists from many countries. The NPS supports these types of cooperative efforts, and endeavors to provide access to NPS lands, information, technical and logistical support, and funding for these types of studies at both the national and international levels to the extent that they can be articulated within existing programs, responsibilities, and missions.

Knowing, understanding, and protecting the archaeological resources of the Americas is our permanent and undivided obligation and one of our most important responsibilities. This will require the cooperation of those who study the resource, those who manage the resource, and those who ultimately support these efforts—the public.

II. The Public Trust

The issue of ownership undoubtedly has perplexed the
animal kingdom since its earliest history. Perhaps it is as old
as the kingdom itself. We know that animals compete for
space and resources at the fundamental level of existence.
Very simple forms of animal life compete for territory and
protect their space by mechanisms ranging from simple to
complex. As animal life becomes more evolved, complex
behaviors protecting the ownership of territory and its
resources move from the individual to the group. To be sure,
we are taught that these behaviors are mechanisms for
survival and can be interpreted as operating at a biological
level. Undoubtedly, humanity has the most evolved, involved, and contradictory concepts of ownership and
property.

Anthropological studies tell us that concepts of ownership
can include not only the material but the nonmaterial. We
know that in some societies real estate, houses, businesses,
ideas, and concepts can be privately held, but that there are
also societies where these same items are owned by the
group or the state. Elsewhere on the face of the earth individuals own or have owned spirits, songs, dances, magical
incantations and the like, but as individuals possess little
material wealth.

In our lifetimes we have seen two politico-economic systems dominate the world. Interestingly, they share fundamental differences in the ownership of property, especially property that is wealth-producing. At this moment we are living in most interesting times as one of these systems peacefully reanalyses some of its fundamental doctrines. Time will provide us with some very interesting events and solutions in this regard.

Universally, irrespective of the prevailing political system, the past, the common history of a nation, is recognized as the common property of the group. To be sure, how that history is developed and the purposes for which the past is used vary, as does the ownership of the material remains of the past. Considering the complexity of concepts of property and ownership, further comments here will be restricted to the general area of archaeology.

In some nations the relics of the past are the property of the state, whereas in others ownership of the cultural relics (and other material evidence of the past) belongs to the landowner, pure and simple. However, this elemental dichotomy in ownership is rare, as papers in this volume show. As with other human endeavors, we tend to create all kinds of exceptions and complexity.

The following paper by Knudson espouses an idea of a universal public trust for the past and its material manifestations. Her ideas are not completely original. Archaeologists have followed their calling out of their personal intellectual needs or wants; most of us have not taken up the shovel and trowel to become rich and famous. I suspect that only after embarking on the study and practice of our trade did we recognize that we were contributing to the grand enterprise of creating knowledge about the undeniable common thread of our humanness. We are indebted to Knudson for a clear presentation of the Public Trust Doctrine. Hopefully, her discourse will serve as a document with which we can persuade others to accept a more responsible vision of their stewardship of the past.

Bennie C. Keel

The Public Trust and Archaeological Stewardship

Ruthann Knudson

In most modern societies, archaeological resources are considered to be part of a worldwide public trust, being joint and severally owned by the members of the human community who all have rights to their heritage information and resources. In this perspective, all people thus have stewardship responsibilities for these rights and these resources, and need to understand, affirm, and implement this ethic. First Americans archaeological resources are a particularly important trust element, because of their rarity and the unique information they contain about humans' adaptation to a pristine New World. Ultimately, governments have archaeological stewardship responsibilities to act on the public's behalf. These responsibilities merit clarification and implementation, but the ethical responsibility belongs first to the average citizen.

Beginning with a leap of faith, as do all ethical positions, I assert that archaeological resources are part of a worldwide public trust, and that they should be used, conserved, and/or destroyed only following consideration of that stewardship responsibility. Some systems of cultural values deny this assertion (see Layton 1989), which I respect, but this discussion focuses on what I believe is a dominant worldwide pattern. Under this scenario, archaeologists have a responsibility to operate as archaeological trustees, as do other members of the public and private world. This is particularly true when dealing with the remains of the First Americans, which are rare, often not surface evident, and hold irreplaceable information about our species' adaptation to a pristine "New World."

A Conceptual Framework

In 1986 I initiated a discussion of contemporary cultural resource management with the question, "Who owns an archaeological site?" (Knudson 1986:395). There was no obvious answer in the United States, nor indeed did there appear to be one elsewhere in the world. In making a comparative study of world cultural resource management systems, Cleere (1984:127) noted that the programs of those countries discussed in his volume generally lacked properly conceived archaeological conservation policies. This is despite the fact that the United Nations Educational, Scientific and Cultural Organization adopted international principles on archaeological excavations in 1956 (UNESCO 1985). Cleere's work reflected the lack of any consistent ethical, much less any formal legal, national policies across the world.

This question of ownership, and consequent stewardship responsibilities, is foremost an ethical issue but, as with most questions of right and wrong and the balance of public and private rights, its implementation is a legal question. A legal system is simply a (usually incomplete) codification of an ethical value system. This paper discusses how the United States has legally addressed my basic ethical affirmation. Subsequent papers will address archaeological resource management in the ethical and legal contexts of other nations.

The basic propositions underlying archaeologists' responsibility for political participation are a universal ethic of public archaeological values:

(1) There is a worldwide moral consensus that the long-term conservation of a significant portion of our cultural past is good for the human community. As a corollary, loss of our nonrenewable heritage resource base engenders significant social cost (Knudson 1984:245).

(2) The long-term goal is conservation of a heritage resource base for the good of the human community, for the preservation of knowledge and objects as they hold value for long-term cultural coherence. It is not conservation of an individual site or building per se, or focus on a specific research topic out of context of its relationship to the overall cultural needs of the human community (Knudson 1984:246; cf. Knecht 1994).

(3) While an important human value, cultural resources (Knudson 1986, forthcoming) are only one aspect of a human social and economic system, and all resource management decisions are made relative to the broader system; to ignore this broad public context is unethical. Thus, archaeological resources should be managed within a more inclusive context

of cultural resources and, further, within the context of national, state, and local public multi-resource policies and programs (Knudson 1984:246).

This set of propositions developed out of the Society for American Archaeology's 1980 Basic Principles of Archaeological Resource Management (Knudson 1982). Implicit within these principles is a public trust concept. Such a concept is also implicit in McGimsey's (1972:5) seminal discussion of public archaeology, and in discussions such as Fowler (1986), Grady and Lipe (1976), Mayer-Oakes (1989), Schaafsma (1989), Tainter and Lucas (1983) in Woodall (1989), and Zelaya (1981). Having a concept label or name—the Public Trust—is an extremely important mnemonic for proselytizing. And we must proselytize, because until there is a clear public ethical consensus about archaeological values we cannot stop the looting and destruction of resources by development forces.

Christopher Chippindale has noted that this concept is not one with which the British are familiar, largely because of the strong modern presumption in European law that landowners' rights are tempered by many other interests (Chippindale 1983). That unfamiliarity and legal difference should not detract from the universal adoption of the ethic and term. In the United States, then-Secretary of the Interior Manuel Lujan, Jr. (1991) promulgated *A National Strategy for Federal Archeology* in which he stated, "[The archaeological paleoenvironmental] record is a public trust to be understood and evaluated to help shape our present responses to changing environments."

The Public Trust Doctrine in U.S. Law

As a U.S. citizen, I have been raised to respect the sanctity of private property rights, with the assumed corollary that archaeological resources are the property of the landowner. But First Americans resources are too valuable to all of us to be treated as either private commodities or treasure. Over the past few years I have discovered that under U.S. water quality laws the public interest often prevails over constitutional Fifth

Amendment property rights. Why not for First Americans archaeological resources as well?

Since 1986, I have attempted to identify the conceptual bases underlying the United States' apparently contrasting legal requirements for the management of archaeological and water resources. This attempt has led me to the Public Trust Doctrine (PTD), an appropriate ethic for worldwide archaeological resource management, though a relatively inchoate set of principles with no clear constitutional basis.

Lipe (1984:2) has cogently pointed out that archaeological cultural resources have value only as those values are assigned by human beings, and that not all such resources have, much less are assigned, equally high value. Archaeological resources are most frequently assigned scientific, humanistic, and spiritual values (Knudson 1991). The Public Trust principle asserts the right of the whole human community to preserve all resources until a value judgment has been made in a manner that best serves the public's broad interests.

The following discussion of the PTD includes a more articulate statement of a worldwide Public Trust principle, an ethical prescript for all private or public individuals or organizations who have some interaction with archaeological resources. The acceptance and implementation of this ethical value is the focus of this discussion and symposium, first in general and secondarily in relation to the First Americans. Its explicit legal codification is a subsidiary issue, as is the issue of compensation of private rights in asserting a public good.

Heritage in today's world is an owned past (see McGuire 1989). It comprises both material property, with actual value in an antiquities market, and information about patrimony and environmental adaptation. We must first ask who owns this heritage, and then, secondarily, who cares for it.

In our contemporary legalistic world community, stewardship rights and responsibilities are explicitly tied to property rights. This linkage of ownership and stewardship is in contrast to some traditional cultural value systems (for instance, Nez Perce mutual cross-utilization stewardship rights and responsibilities [Walker 1967]). The public nature of archaeological resources, and the obligation of governments, private individuals, and organizations to fulfill their responsibilities as trustees of these public resources, merits broader recognition and affirmation.

In 1970, Joseph Sax published a seminal paper on the PTD in U.S. natural resource law. Natural resource law is different from environmental law in that the former usually refers to the resource consumer and the latter to the resource protector (Freedman 1987:66). Archaeological resource management, like minerals management, falls between these two categories when it is directed to the conservative consumption of a nonrenewable resource base (cf. Lipe 1974, Thompson 1974). U.S. federal archaeological laws (e.g., Antiquities Act of 1906, Archeological and Historic Preservation Act of 1974, Archaeological Resources Protection Act) are environmental rather than natural resource laws, prescriptive reactions to threats of damage and destruction. There is no archaeological resource law that is a proactive statement of management policy (see Douglas, this volume).

Sax (1970:476) pointed out that while the PTD had its origins in the Roman Justinian Code and in Magna Carta property rights in rivers, seas, and the shore,

> Of all the concepts known to American law, only the public trust doctrine seems to have the breadth and substantive content which might make it useful as a tool for general application by citizens seeking to develop a comprehensive legal approach to resource management problems (Sax 1970:474).

Basically the PTD is a mixture of ideas that have been set forth in U.S. case law since 1821 (Stevens 1980:199), focusing on Sax's (1970:484) concept

> . . . that there are certain interests that are intrinsically so important to every citizen that their free availability tends to mark the society as one of citizens rather than serfs; to protect these, it is necessary to be especially wary so no individual or group acquires power to control them.

Sax (1970:485) went on to note that private use of these publicly significant resources is often so inappropriate that an individual land surface title owner can only have usufruct ownership of those resources, and hence must recognize the public nature of archaeological resources which happen to be on this property. Huffman (1986:571) argues that this may be true for water because of its migratory nature, but probably is not applicable to nonmigratory resources. However, no one has explored the concept's legal application to heritage resources, much less its explicit ethical statement.

Property is "that which is peculiar or proper to any person . . . an aggregate of rights which are guaranteed or protected by the government" (Black 1979). The essence of property law is respect for a property holder's reasonable expectations that her or his rights can be exercised (Reich 1964, Sax 1980:186-187). It is asserted here that the world's entire population has a right to information about its human heritage (cf. California Heritage Task Force 1984:24, Di Stefano 1988) and therefore all members of the human community are joint and severally owners of all archaeological resources, no matter the ownership status of the depositional context of those resources. It is thus a logical corollary that each government or private individual with legal jurisdiction over the physical context of archaeological deposits has a trust responsibility to protect the joint ownership rights of the entire human community. A further corollary is that all site discoverers have such a responsibility.

The PTD is not explicitly recognized in the U.S. Constitution or its original supporting documents (Huffman 1986:579, Kammen 1986). Its implicit statement has been tied to the Ninth Amendment—"The enumeration in the Constitution, of certain rights, shall not be construed to deny or disparage others retained by the people"—as a "right to a decent environment" (Freedman 1987:32-35, Sloan 1979:63; cf. Adler 1988).

The PTD has also been tied (Sax 1980, Wilkinson 1980:311) to the Property Clause of the U.S. Constitution (Art. IV, Sec. 3, Para. 2):

> The Congress shall have Power to dispose of and make all needful Rules and Regulations respecting the

> Territory or other Property belonging to the United
> States. . . .

However, the Property Clause has been only infrequently applied to the regulation of private property (Reed 1986, Shepard 1984), and more often such regulation has relied on what is generally known as the "police power" to regulate public nuisances (Grad 1971:1-15, Humbach 1987:561, Sax 1964).

In addition, the Fourteenth Amendment—

> . . . No State shall make or enforce any law which shall
> abridge the privileges or immunities of citizens of the
> United States; nor shall any State deprive any person of
> life, liberty, or property, without due process of law;
> nor deny to any person within its jurisdiction the equal
> protection of the laws (Sec. 1).

—has been cited as a basis for the PTD.

Some states (California, New Jersey, Illinois, Wisconsin, Florida, Louisiana, Massachusetts, North Dakota, and Oregon) have expressly codified the PTD in relation to specified natural resources (Huffman 1986:572, Wilson 1984). In Louisiana, this specifically includes the "healthful, scenic, historic and aesthetic quality of the environment" (Freedman 1987:230).

Until recently, there had been little explicit legal confrontation between the PTD and the taking issue or Just Compensation Clause of the Fifth Amendment (Bosselman et al. 1973, though see Reagan 1988, U.S. Department of the Interior Solicitor 1979). That Amendment states that no property shall be taken for public use without due compensation. There clearly have been ethical confrontations between the two perspectives, as in archaeological mining of private lands. Similarly, there are conflicts between surface ownership rights and the rights of American Indians in the disposition of Indian human remains and associated funerary items (Price 1991:23-24).

Humbach (1987:551-553) points out that there are two types of property interests that can be taken: property *rights* (legal advantage an owner has because of legal duties imposed on others [e.g., no trespass]) and property *freedoms* (legal advantage of being able to do what one wants on one's property).

The Supreme Court has rarely required compensation of *freedom* takings such as may occur through general zoning, although Executive Order 12630 states that such governmental actions may require compensation (Reagan 1988:347). However, new scholarly attention is being paid to the social benefits of common ownership of natural resources (McCay and Acheson 1987), and the tradeoffs in balancing property rights and justice (Goldfarb 1988, Sagoff 1988). Former U.S Supreme Court Justice William J. Brennan, who was most influential in rulings on historic building preservation vs. private property rights, held to the following land use proposition:

> Although the individual's right to develop and use
> private property may be severely limited by rights of
> the community, the individual in all events is entitled
> to an expectation of reasonable economic use and must
> receive compensation for loss of value if a regulation
> goes too far (Haar and Kayden 1991:15).

And further:

> We must distinguish those property "rights" that relate
> to the use, enjoyment, privacy, the right to enforce
> trespass, and the right to dispose of and inherit land
> from the "right" to gain the highest and immediate
> dollar return based on expectancy or speculative value
> (Collins 1991; cf Weber 1991).

There is undeniable ethical and legal tension between these two concepts, and each governmental and private landowner decision about resource use must involve a case-specific balancing of competing uses (Stevens 1980:223). There is a need to reconcile the Public Trust with a community's right to the benefits of private ownership (Wilson 1984:897). But, as John Gardner (1960:23) has noted:

> Our pluralistic philosophy invites each organization,
> institution, or special group to develop and enhance its
> own potentialities. *But the price of that treasured au-*
> *tonomy and self-preoccupation is that each institution*
> *concern itself also with the common good.* This is not
> idealism; it is self-preservation [italics in the original].

Application of the PTD to U.S. historic architectural properties has been a special issue since the Supreme Court *Penn Central* case in 1978, which rendered a decision that

> . . . stands for the proposition that the rights incident to property ownership are not absolute, but are subject to reasonable regulation for the benefit of the community without the necessity of requiring the public to pay monetary compensation [Doheny 1993:8].

Recently, Joseph Sax has addressed the application of the PTD to the preservation of historic properties, asserting that "Property rights claims do not stand as a significant barrier to protection of cultural properties" (Sax 1993:137). When U.S. courts consider the conflict between individual freedom and the values of a community with either a shared culture or diverse cultures within the larger society, over time they have quietly supported the protection of heritage values.

The U.S. courts continue to refine the judicial interpretation of the Fifth Amendment Just Compensation Clause (Harper 1994, Roddewig 1993), and there continues to be considerable misunderstanding in the United States of the difference between property rights and property values (Rypkema 1993). The built environment community within the U.S. historic preservation program has recently articulated more carefully its belief in the appropriateness of applying the PTD to that program. Recent papers relate historic preservation to civic responsibilities for stewardship, managing the impact of change on people and their environment and value conflicts between individuals and community (Beaumont 1993); to open space protection (Dehart and Frobouck 1993); and to quality of life (Lewis 1993). To date these discussions have addressed the application of the PTD only to submerged archaeological resources (Denton et al. 1993), and not broader issues, much less the archaeological resources of indigenous people (cf. Brush 1993). All First Americans scholars and other enthusiasts have a responsibility to participate in the application of the Public Trust concept to the full range of cultural (Hufford 1990, 1994) and natural heritage resources, including the built environment.

In October 1993, a "carefully planned, no-holds-barred strategy session" was held in Sundance, Utah, to address the takings issue, the participants being western U.S. state legislators, environmental and conservation leaders, environmental lobbyists, and union leaders (MacWilliams Cosgrove Snider 1994). While First Americans preservation concerns were not discussed specifically, the Sundance Conference and coalition are an appropriate sociopolitical forum in which to address those concerns.

Before archaeological sites on public or private lands can consistently be the subject of public decisions, their membership within an inalienable public trust must be recognized by both archaeologists and non-archaeologists. This change must be complemented by a change in the public's perception of archaeology's intrinsic nature and values.

Stewardship

Stewardship has been used to stand for archaeological site protection and conservation in the United States for at least the past two decades; it may have been common earlier, but I was not familiar with it. The dictionary defines *steward* as "a person who manages another's property or financial affairs, or who administers anything as the agent of another or others" (Stein 1975:1289). In using the term, archaeologists implicitly affirm that archaeological resources are someone's property without dealing explicitly with the concepts of ownership rights and responsibilities. These must be addressed before the question of who manages the property, and how is it to be done, can be adequately addressed.

My initial assertion included the concept of a public *trust*, not just a public interest. Identifying something as being in the public's interest is a statement of a collective ethic, but has no enforcement mechanism. Who are going to be the stewards of this public interest? The concept of a Public Trust requires an agent of action, a trustee of the public interest.

While I believe archaeological resources have more scientific, humanistic, and spiritual value than generally is perceived, their apparent inertness and inability to do work means that the average citizen sees them as curiosities but not a significant factor in tradeoffs that do have economic benefit (Knudson 1989a). At present, the average citizen is unlikely to be a steward of archaeological resources or the public rights related to them. In the long run there probably is a need for legal codification of the Public Trust concept as it applies to archaeological resources. First, though, archaeologists and other concerned citizens must affirm and articulate the concept of people as public trustees, to enhance informal stewardship. Acceptance of this ethic will in turn develop a constituency for a possibly necessary future political campaign. And, secondarily but before codification, the economic benefits and costs of archaeological management and consumption must be articulated to provide a valid basis for debates over tradeoffs and compensation (Schmid 1989; cf. Cantor 1991, Chappelle and Webster 1993, Lutz 1993, Tietenberg 1992; see Knudson forthcoming).

Manuel Lujan, Jr. , U.S. Secretary of the Interior from 1988 to 1992, established a ten-point agenda for the department under the theme of STEWARDSHIP (Greenberg 1989). The focus was originally on natural resources, but in 1991 the Secretary promulgated his *National Strategy for Federal Archeology* (Lujan 1991), complementing his earlier agenda. It is imperative that the archaeological community continue to educate its political leaders about the need to keep a stewardship focus on our cultural resources.

Most important to effective archaeological stewardship is the public's perception of the public trust, including private landowners' participation in archaeological resource management across the country and world. Conservation of archaeological sites in place, or collection of information and artifacts excavated to allow other resource uses, while considering the private interests of related individuals, is responsible execution of a public trust. It can bring benefits by contributing scientific knowledge (often about issues such as waste management methods and desired future ecosystem conditions as well as about cultural heritage), heritage continuities, good public relations, recreation, or tourism opportunities.

First Americans Resources within the Public Trust

First Americans archaeological resources are an irreplaceable record of human adaptation to a pristine natural New World, one not modified by oil spills, nuclear waste, municipal land-fills, or acid rain. Interdisciplinary studies such as those described throughout this conference provide a unique record of human technological and sociocultural growth and development and paleoenvironmental conditions. They can provide a significant database for better understanding relationships between people and their environment in the Artic, which has been identified as a top priority by the Committee on Arctic Social Sciences (1989). They can provide similar information in other environments, and in the broadest studies of global climatic and ecological change (cf. Earth System Sciences Committee 1988, Malone and Corell 1989:33). Nuclear waste must be disposed of to be safe for 10,000 years; most people have no concept of 10,000 years, much less how to design engineered systems that provide that safety. Archaeological studies can do work in areas such as these, if archaeologists understand the questions that need to be addressed, and can help to search for some answers while doing personally satisfying research.

First Americans resources are relatively rare, often not sur-face evident, and often do not include such spectacular features or artifacts that they acquire an immediate public fan club. They can be conserved only within a Public Trust concept.

Summary and Conclusions

Archaeological resources are part of a public trust, being joint and severally owned by the members of the universal human community. Affirmative stewardship of all archaeological materials must include archaeological education of the general public, politicians, Native Americans, and other interest groups in addition to, if not before, the physical management of the sites and artifacts.

Archaeology also needs to be recognized as part of the general environmental management equation, because of its public nature as part of a trust managed by both private individuals and governments, before there are no sites left about which to worry (Knudson 1989b). At the same time, the U.S. Fifth and Fourteenth Amendments concerning property rights need to be addressed in specific multiresource management decisions that involve archaeology. U.S. society is based on the generation of wealth through the use of natural resources that are themselves also elements of the public trust; resource management is thus always a balancing of competing goals and interests.

Acknowledgments

I am indebted to Roger Ryman, retired Manager, Land and Environment, Shell Pipe Line Company, who first forced me to confront the issue of archaeological site ownership and management responsibility when I was working with him on the Cortez Pipeline project. Steven E. James, Vice President, Woodward-Clyde Consultants, led me to the concept of the Public Trust Doctrine. The University of Idaho College of Law Library was invaluable in my background research on the doctrine, and Arthur D. Smith, Jr., Associate Dean of the College, was an interested supporter of that research. Subsequent participation in the 1990 Cultural Conservation Conference sponsored by the American Folklife Center, U.S. Library of Congress, Washington; the 1991 annual meeting of the National Association of Environmental Professionals in Baltimore; and 1992-1993 discussions on property rights and historic preservation with Preservation Action and the National Trust for Historic Preservation, Washington, have been invaluable in assisting me to understand the context of how the PTD can be implemented.

References Cited

Adler, M.J.
1988 We Hold These Truths. *The Commonwealth* 82:108-111.

Beaumont, C.E.
1993 Property Rights and Civic Responsibilities. *Historic Preservation Forum* 7(4):30-35.

Black, H.C.
1979 *Black's Dictionary* (5th ed.). West Publishing Company, St. Paul.

Bosselman, F., D. Callies, and J. Banta
1973 *The Taking Issue.* Council on Environmental Quality, Washington.

Brush, S.B.
1993 Indigenous Knowledge of Biological Resources and Intellectual Property Rights: The Role of Anthropology. *American Anthropologist* 95:653-686.

California Heritage Task Force
1984 *California Heritage Task Force.* A Report to the Legislature and People of California. California Heritage Task Force, Sacramento.

Cantor, R.
1991 Beyond the Market: Recent Regulatory Responses to the Externalities of Energy Production. *Proceedings of the 1991 Conference of the National Association of Environmental Professionals*, edited by D.B. Hunsaker, Jr., and G.F. Kelman, pp. G51 through G61. National Association of Environmental Professionals, Washington.

Chappelle, D.E., and H.H. Webster
1993 Consistent Valuation of Natural Resource Outputs to Advance Both Economic Development and Environmental Protection. *Renewable Resources Journal* 11(4):14-17.

Chippindale, C.
1983 The Making of the First Ancient Monuments Act, 1882, and its Administration under General Pitt-Rivers. *Journal of the British Archaeological Association* 136:1-55.

Cleere, H.
1984 World Cultural Resource Management: Problems and Perspectives. In *Approaches to the Archaeological Heritage*, edited by H. Cleere, pp. 125-131. Cambridge University Press, Cambridge.

Collins, R.C.
1991 Land Use Ethics and Property Rights. *Journal of Soil and Water Conservation* 46(6):417-418.

Committee on Arctic Social Sciences
1989 *Arctic Social Science: An Agenda for Action.* Committee on Arctic Social Sciences, Polar Research Board, Commission on Physical Sciences, Mathematics, and Resources, National Research Council, Washington.

Dehart, H.G., and J.A. Frobouck
1993 Preserving Public Interests and Property Rights. *Historic Preservation Forum* 7(4):36-46.

Denton, S., C.A. Shafer, and L.L. Leighty
1993 The Public Trust Doctrine: How May It Apply to Shipwrecks and Other Underwater Cultural Resources? In *Great Lakes Underwater Cultural Resources: Important Information for Shaping Our Future,* edited by K.J. Vrana and E. Mahoney, Appendix C. Department of Park and Recreation Resources, Michigan State University, East Lansing.

Di Stefano, R.
1988 Editorial. *ICOMOS Information,* No. 3 (1988).

Doheny, D.A.
1993 Property Rights and Historic Preservation. *Historic Preservation Forum* 7(4):77-10.

Earth System Sciences Committee, NASA Advisory Council
1988 *Earth System Science: A Program for Global Change.* National Aeronautics and Space Administration, Washington.

Fowler, D.F.
1986 Conserving American Archaeological Resources. In *American Archaeology Past and Future,* edited by D.J. Meltzer, D.D. Fowler, and J.A Sabloff, pp. 135-162. Smithsonian Institution Press, Washington.

Freedman, W.
1987 *Hazardous Waste Liability.* The Michie Company, Charlottesville, Virginia.

Gardner, J.
1960 *Leadership: a Sampler of the Wisdom of John Gardner.* Hubert H. Humphrey Institute of Public Affairs, University of Minnesota, Minneapolis.

Goldfarb, W.
1988 Litigation and Legislation: Takings and the Public Trust Doctrine. *Water Resources Bulletin* 24:1133-1134.

Grad, F.P.
1971 *Environmental Law*. Matthew Bender, New York.

Grady, M., and W. Lipe
1976 The Role of Preservation in Conservation Archaeology. *American Society for Conservation Archaeology Proceedings 1976*: 1-11.

Greenberg, R.M. (editor)
1989 Stewardship of America's Public Lands and Natural Resources. *CRM Bulletin* 12(1):24.

Haar, C.M., and J.S. Kayden
1991 *Landmark Justice. The Influence of William J. Brennan on America's Communities*. The Preservation Press, Washington.

Harper, L.A.
1994 A New View of Regulatory Takings? *Environment* 36(1):2-5,39-40.

Huffman, J.L.
1986 Trusting the Public Interest to Judges: A Comment on the Public Trust Writings of Professors Sax, Wilkinson, Dunning, and Johnson. *Denver University Law Review* 63:565-584.

Hufford, M.
1990 Reconfiguring the Cultural Mission: A Report on the First National Cultural Conservation Conference. *Folklife Center News* 7(3-4):3-7.

———— (editor)
1994 *Conserving Culture: A New Discourse on Heritage*. University of Illinois Press, Urbana.

Humbach, J.A.
1987 Constitutional Limits on the Power to Take Private Property: Public Purpose and Public Use.*Oregon Law Review* 66:547-598.

Kammen, M. (editor)
1986 *The Origins of the American Constitution*. Penguin Books, New York.

Knecht, R.
1994 Archaeology and Alutiiq Cultural Identity on Kodiak Island. *Society for American Archaeology Bulletin* 12(5): 8-10.

Knudson, R.
1982 Basic Principles of Archaeological Resource Management. *American Antiquity* 47(1):163-166.

1984 Ethical Decision Making and Participation in the Politics of Archaeology. In *Ethics and Values in Archaeology*, edited by E.L. Green, pp. 243-263. The Free Press, Collier-Macmillan, New York.

1986 Contemporary Cultural Resource Management. In *American Archaeology Past and Present*, edited by D.J. Meltzer, D.D. Fowler, and J.B. Sabloff, pp. 395-413. Smithsonian Institution Press, Washington.

1991 The Archaeological Public Trust in Context. In *Protecting the Past*, edited by G.S. Smith and J.E. Ehrenhard, pp. 3-8. CRC Press, Boca Raton, Florida.

Forthcoming. Cultural Resources in the 1990s. In *Advances in Science and Technology for Historic Preservation [Advances in Archaeological and Museum Science Series]*, edited by R.A. Williamson. Plenum Corporation, New York.

Layton, R. (editor)
1989 *Conflict in the Archaeology of Living Traditions*. Unwin Hyman, London.

Lewis, T.A.
1993 Property Rights and Human Rights. *Historic Preservation Forum* 7(4):47-51.

Lipe, W.D.
1974 A Conservation Model for American Archaeology. *Kiva* 39:213-245.

1984 Value and Meaning in Cultural Resources. In *Approaches to the Archaeological Heritage*, edited by H. Cleere, pp. 1-11. Cambridge University Press, Cambridge.

Lujan, Jr., M.
1991 A National Strategy for Federal Archeology. Policy Statement, Secretary of the Interior, U.S. Department of the Interior, Washington. (Reprinted, *SAA Bulletin* 10:10,15 [1992].)

Lutz, E. (editor)
1993 *Toward Improved Accounting for the Environment*. The World Bank, Washington.

MacWilliams Cosgrove Snider
1994 *The Sundance Conference. Rocky Mountain States "Takings" Strategy Meeting*. Americans for the Environment, Washington.

Malone, T.R., and R. Corell
1989 Mission to Planet Earth Revisited. *Environment* 31:6-11,31-35.

Mayer-Oakes, W.J.
1989 Science, Service, and Stewardship—A Basis for the Ideal
Archaeology of the Future. In *Archaeological Heritage Management
in the Modern World*, edited by H.F. Cleere, pp. 52-58. Unwin
Hyman, London.

McCay, B.J., and J.M. Acheson (editors)
1987 *The Culture and Ecology of Communal Resources*. University of
Arizona Press, Tucson.

McGimsey, C.R. III
1972 *Public Archaeology*. Seminar Press, New York.

McGuire, R.H.
1989 Archaeology and the Vanishing American. *First Joint
Archaeological Congress, Abstracts*:141. Baltimore, Maryland.

Price, H.M., III
1991 *Disputing the Dead. U.S. Law on Aboriginal Remains and Grave
Goods*. University of Missouri Press, Columbia.

Reagan, R.
1988 Executive Order 12630—Governmental Actions and
Interference With Constitutionally Protected Property Rights.
March 16, 1988. *Administration of Ronald Reagan, 1988*: 347-350.

Reed, S.W.
1986 The Public Trust Doctrine: Is It Amphibious? *Journal of
Environmental Law and Litigation* 1:107-122.

Reich, C.
1964 The New Property. *Yale Law Journal* 73:33ff.

Roddewig, R.J.
1993 Historic Preservation and the Constitution. *Historic
Preservation Forum* 7(4):11-22.

Rypkema, D.D.
1993 Property Rights/Property Values. *Historic Preservation Forum*
7(4):23-29.

Sagoff, M.
1988 Environmental Protection and Property Rights. *Forum for
Applied Research and Public Policy* 3:75-84.

Sax, J.L.
1964 Takings and the Police Power. *Yale Law Journal* 74:36-76.

1970 The Public Trust Doctrine in Natural Resource Law: Effective
Judicial Intervention. *Michigan Law Review* 68:471-566.

1980 Liberating the Public Trust Doctrine From Its Historical
Shackles. *U.C. Davis Law Review* 14:185-194.

1993 Property Rights and Public Benefits. In *Past Meets Future:
Saving America's Historic Environments*, edited by A.J. Lee, pp.
137-143. The Preservation Press, Washington.

Schaafsma, C.F.
1989 Significant Until Proven Otherwise: Problems Versus
Representative Samples. In *Archaeological Heritage Management in
the Modern World, edited by H.F. Cleere*, pp. 38-51. Unwin Hyman,
London.

Schmid, A.A.
1989 *Benefit-Cost Analysis: A Political Economy Approach*. Westview
Press, Boulder, Colorado.

Shepard, B.
1984 The Scope of Congress' Constitutional Power Under the
Property Clause: Regulating Non-Federal Property to Further
the Purposes of National Parks and Wilderness Areas. *Boston
College Environmental Affairs*, 11:479-538.

Sloan, I.J.
1979 *Environment and the Law*. Oceana Publications, Inc., Dobbs
Ferry, New York.

Stein, J. (editor-in-chief)
1975 *The Random House College Dictionary*, rev. ed. Random House,
Inc., New York.

Stevens, J.S.
1980 The Public Trust: A Sovereign's Ancient Prerogatives Become
the People's Environmental Right. *U.C. Davis Law Review* 14:195-
232.

Tainter, J.A., and G.J. Lucas
1983 Epistemology of the Significance Concept. *American Antiquity*
48:707-719.

Thompson, R.H.
1974 Institutional Responsibilities in Conservation Archaeology. In
Proceedings of the 1974 Cultural Resource Management Conference,
edited by W.D. Lipe and A.J. Lindsay, Jr., pp. 13-24. Museum of
Northern Arizona - Technical Series No. 14.

Tietenberg, T.
1992 *Environmental and Natural Resource Economics*. 3rd ed.
HarperCollins Publishers Inc., New York.

United Nations Educational, Scientific and Cultural Organization
(UNESCO)
1985 [1983] Recommendation on International Principles
    Applicable to Archeological Excavations. In *Conventions and
    Recommendations of Unesco Concerning the Protection of the Cultural
    Heritage*, pp. 101-115. United Nations Educational, Scientific and
    Cultural Organization, Paris.

U.S. Department of the Interior Solicitor
1979 The Extent to Which the National Historic Preservation Act
    Requires Cultural Resources to be Identified and Considered in
    the Grant of a Federal Right-of-Way. Memorandum to the
    Secretary of the Interior, December 6, 1979. U.S. Department of
    the Interior, Washington.

Walker, D.E., Jr.
1967 Mutual Cross-Utilization of Economic Resources in the
    Plateau: An Example from Aboriginal Nez Perce Fishing
    Practices. *Washington State University Laboratory of Anthropology
    Reports of Investigation* No. 41.

Weber, L.J.
 1991 The Social Responsibility of Land Ownership. *Journal of
    Forestry* 89(4):12-25.

Wilkinson, C.F.
1980 The Public Trust Doctrine in Public Land Law. *U.C. Davis Law
    Review* 14(2):269-316.

Wilson, H.J.
1984 The Public Trust Doctrine in Massachusetts Land Law. *Boston
    College Environmental Affairs Law Rev.* 11(4):839-899.

Woodall, J.N. (editor)
1989 *Predicaments, Pragmatics, and Professionalism: Ethical Conduct in
    Archeology.* Special Publication No. 1. Society of Professional
    Archeologists, Oklahoma City.

Zelaya, J.L.
1982 The OAS as Preserver of the Cultural Heritage. In *Rescue
    Archeology: Papers from the First New World Conference on Rescue
    Archeology*, edited by R.L. Wilson and G. Loyola, pp. 11-17. The
    Preservation Press, Washington.

III. Research Guidance

The focus of the First World Summit Conference on the Peopling of the Americas was current research in First Americans studies, and those papers are presented in detail in four other proceedings volumes. A second conference theme was the public context in which First Americans resources are studied, used, managed, and destroyed. The following paper by Bonnichsen et al. is a summary of current and future First Americans research needs in that context of public management.

Bennie C. Keel

Future Directions in First Americans Research and Management

Robson Bonnichsen, Tom D. Dillehay, George C. Frison, Fumiko Ikawa-Smith, Ruthann Knudson, D. Gentry Steele, Allan R. Taylor, & John Tomenchuk

First Americans research has come of age and provides primary data important for understanding local, regional, and global dynamics and linkages among past climates, ecologies, and human adaptations. Better site reports and analytical hypotheses need to be developed, along with standardized classification and descriptive techniques. Bioanthropological studies need to make better use of the available sample of early modern human skeletal material, and to develop more accurate models of biological relationships. Additional methods, relying on statistics and various kinds of typologies, are needed to deal with linguistic resemblances to evaluate relationships among indigenous American and Asian populations, and South American languages need to be documented more fully. The traditional link between scholarly and public archaeology needs to be re-established, because public land and resource management is the context for First Americans resource management and research in North America and other nations. Public outreach and archaeological education are vital elements in conservation and continued study of First Americans resources, and the Native American community should be more involved in First Americans study. The coming of age of First Americans research involves affirmative partnerships with other public and private stewards of the heritage public trust.

As we stand at the threshold of the twenty-first century, our world is a global village. Sophisticated information technologies provided by satellite imagery, electronic communication, and computer technology are profoundly affecting how we perceive, analyze, and comprehend the world around us. In the global village, we are becoming more aware of our individual responsibilities as scholars of publicly valued archaeological information, and as managers of publicly valued archaeological materials.

With the development of space-age technology, we are now not only capable of gaining an even more comprehensive understanding of how the earth and its cultures function, but also of probing the remote past and developing a more realistic understanding of the origin and dispersal of modern humans. Central to this endeavor is archaeology's great unanswered question of when and how the Americas were initially peopled. A definitive answer to this global problem is not yet in hand, though a number of significant scientific advances have been made over the last two decades. Yet most people are unaware of these advances.

Developing and integrating into society scientific knowledge about our human heritage involves research, conservation, and public education, as well as public policy to guide and integrate these components. As a major step in this process, the Center for the Study of the First Americans (CSFA) convened the First World Summit Conference on the Peopling of the Americas during May 1989 (Summit '89) to synthesize scientific knowledge about early American origins. Scientific research specialists from Asia, North America, and South America participated in the conference and have contributed papers for four edited volumes relating to method and theory, the Ice Age prehistory of North America and South America, and the Ice Age environments and the prehistory of Asia (Bonnichsen and Steele 1994, Bonnichsen et al. forthcoming (a) and (b), Bonnichsen and Dillehay forthcoming). Within Summit '89, a symposium, "The Public Trust and the First Americans," focused on the public legal and educational environments necessary to support research on the Americas' earliest cultural heritage, conserve First Americans resources, and educate the world's peoples about this unique legacy. This volume includes the special symposium proceedings, and this paper summarizes the scientific and public context of the conference in which the discussions of public responsibility occurred.

Scientific research drives the development of new knowledge. Yet often, as in the case of First Americans studies, many important results are not disseminated to other scientists, integrated into resource management practices, or made available to the public and school educators. Building from results of information developed in conjunction with Summit '89, the purpose of this paper is to: (1) outline potential future research directions important to understanding the origin and spread of Ice Age peoples and their cultures into the Americas;

(2) discuss public stewardship issues important to preserving and conserving fragile First Americans cultural and natural resources; and (3) outline the need for enhanced public education programs to inform the world about the importance of our human heritage.

Scholarly Frontiers

Recent world events, particularly the opening of China and the end of the Cold War, make this an opportune time to formulate a global vision of First Americans studies that embraces Asia, North America, and South America.

Development of knowledge about early American human populations is important to the anthropological subdisciplines of sociocultural anthropology, archaeology, linguistics, and physical and applied anthropology. Data provided by First Americans research are essential for the development of theories to explain the mechanisms involved in the dispersal of human populations and variation among biological populations, languages, and sociocultural patterns inferred from the archaeological record. They are important to Native Americans' identification of heritage values for incorporation within education and cultural maintenance programs. First Americans research provides the framework for understanding later periods of environmental adaptation and cultural development in American prehistory, history, and contemporary society.

The field of early-human research in the New World has come of age. First Americans research does not simply contribute to anthropological or historical problems; it provides primary data important for understanding local, regional, and global issues relevant to explaining the dynamics and linkages among paleoclimatic, geologic, paleoecologic, and human adaptive systems and changes in these linked systems through time.

Archaeology and Quaternary Sciences

Rather than advocating a single perspective or model, we outline philosophical considerations important to developing a systematic knowledge of America's early prehistory. Archaeological field research, which produces the primary scientific data for reconstructing America's early cultural heritage, has become increasingly sophisticated in using a multidisciplinary approach. By drawing upon the allied disciplines of archaeology and the Quaternary sciences, researchers now have a multiplicity of specialized tools at their disposal for reconstructing how people lived in past environments, as well as the means for investigating human response to rapidly changing environmental circumstances.

Much new information documenting regional environmental and archaeological records from Asia, North America, and South America is now, or soon will be, available (Agenbroad et al. 1990, Bonnichsen and Dillehay forthcoming, Bonnichsen and Sorg 1989, Bonnichsen and Steele forthcoming, Bonnichsen and Turnmire 1991, Bonnichsen et al. forthcoming (a), Bonnichsen et al. forthcoming (b), Bryan 1986, Carlisle 1988, Dillehay and Meltzer 1991, Dillehay et al. 1992, Mead and Meltzer 1985, Nunez and Meggers 1987, Stanford and Day 1991, Tankersley and Isaac 1990). Despite this growing volume of quality information, our understanding of early American prehistory remains amazingly sketchy and even the best defined regional patterns are poorly known. For example, the Clovis complex of the United States has received greater scientific attention than any other early regional pattern in the country, and popular writers have characterized this pattern as produced by spear-wielding mammoth hunters. Yet we do not have a firm understanding of (1) the antecedents of this pattern, (2) the organizational dynamics of Clovis sociocultural groups, (3) the factors responsible for regional variation of fluted point assemblages, (4) whether Clovis represents one or several cultural groups, or (5) what led to the demise or transformation of this pattern to other forms.

Early American archaeological complexes are usually distinguished by unique and diagnostic projectile point styles.

These styles are assumed to have been produced by, and thus to archaeologically identify, different sociocultural groups of prehistoric people. Such complexes include the Nenana of Alaska with its lanceolate projectile points (Goebel et al. 1991), the Paleoarctic pattern with wedge-shaped microblade cores (Clark 1991), the Goshen with its concave-based lanceolate points (Frison 1991), the Western Pluvial Lake with its long lanceolate points (Bryan 1991), the El Jobo with its bullet-shaped lanceolates (Bryan 1991, Gruhn 1991), and the fishtail point complex with its stemmed fluted points (Politis 1991). However, our understanding of the organizational and distributional variability of these various complexes is poor, as is our understanding of the simple core and flake tool patterns of South America (Bryan 1991, Gruhn 1991). It should come as no surprise that relationships among regional archaeological records are often ambiguous and have mitigated against widespread acceptance of general models of human migration which seek to explain the peopling of the Americas.

Several impediments have stood in the way of developing a systematic knowledge of the First Americans. It has been difficult for widely dispersed researchers, isolated by language barriers, to be aware of and to assimilate research results from outside of their own nations. Research is often guided by dissimilar standards and results are often not comparable from one report to the next. Available financial resources are unevenly distributed among nations. Consequently, research on the peopling of the Americas has developed in an uneven and piecemeal fashion.

A broader perspective is needed to offset a common bias in Paleoindian research—a bias toward viewing chronologies and other ideas developed in the U.S. Southwest and Great Plains as appropriate as a basis for interpreting records from other areas. Scholars traditionally have approached the peopling of the Americas by attempting to explain local and regional archaeological records. Rather than extrapolating results from one area to another, the case for America's earliest cultural heritage should be developed by encouraging the production of quality site reports from many areas with detailed data presentation that draw on the full complement of allied disciplines embraced by the Quaternary sciences including anthropology. Quality site reports are vital for developing a systematic knowledge of Late Pleistocene archaeological and environmental records from Asia, South America, and North America. These data can, in turn, be synthesized and used for constructing viable models of early American prehistory.

A basic problem with early humans research is that it is too dependent upon inductive interpretation. Although this complaint may seem old, a strong argument can be made for more problem-oriented research than that done by most First Americans contributors. The goal of understanding the organizing principles responsible for migration, colonization, adaptation, and possible linkages with natural environmental changes is a far more difficult and time-consuming type of science than is developing a phase sequence or excavating a single site presumed to be representative of a culture or subculture. To view a culture as a mobile niche-filling system calls for archaeologists to structure their research within a problem framework.

Well-formulated hypotheses about (1) the dynamics governing the rise, operations, and demise of past societies; (2) the causes responsible for migration and colonization; and (3) linkages between environmental and cultural changes are needed to focus and invigorate this field of investigation. This will also require a focus on specific, usually local, problems or sets of closely related problems of significance. Because of the multidisciplinary nature of data at archaeological sites, each of us must be aware of problems of concern to other scientists and of the data demands of addressing those problems. The development of viable multidisciplinary research designs for data recovery must be tempered by the kinds of data present, available time and money, and the desire to obtain and report representative samples of all types of data present at a site. And, if possible, the data demands of as-yet-undefined future problems must be anticipated.

A number of needs must be met in fulfilling the goal of preparing better site reports and developing hypotheses important for interpreting local, regional, and global problems.

1. To evaluate the appropriateness of assumptions employed in making inferences about specific archaeological sites and the natural environments in which they occurred. For example, it would be useful to evaluate the appropriateness of *basic* assumptions, such as: (1) there was a universal Paleoindian stage; (2) there were vast migrations during the Pleistocene/Holocene transition; and (3) the initial peopling of Beringia required an Upper Paleolithic level of technology.

In the process of developing analogues for interpreting the past, we must be keenly aware that the dynamics and linkages among the earth's oceanographic, atmospheric, climatic, glaciologic, geologic, and biotic systems have not been constant through time (Ruddiman and Wright 1987). Contemporary paleoclimatological research suggests that the linkages among the earth's environmental subsystems were discretely different during glacial and interglacial times (Broeker and Denton 1990a, 1990b). The transition from glacial to interglacial periods is thought to have been abrupt and to have been synchronous world-wide. The precise mechanisms responsible for transitions between glacial and interglacial environmental systems are not fully understood and are being researched actively.

Of particular importance to the peopling of the Americas is the issue of how humans respond to abrupt climate change. The change at the Pleistocene/Holocene boundary is postulated to have had a dramatic impact on the world's landscapes. The amount of available glacial ice was significantly reduced; sea levels rose, drowning former shorelines; temperature and precipitation patterns changed; the amount and distribution of surface water was greatly altered; and the structures of plant and animal communities were significantly modified. Although considerable effort is being made to understand the dynamics of how the last Ice Age ended, we also need to understand how glacial and interstadial periods begin and terminate. There can be little doubt that these linked events dramatically affected the ways humans related to the natural environment.

Archaeological research on human adaptations to Holocene environments provides us with a wealth of information on the array of adaptive patterns devised in response to the most recent interglacial environment. However, our knowledge of human adaptations to glacial and interstadial environments is limited by a sparse and fragmentary archaeological record.

We lack modern analogues for understanding how humans responded to global environmental changes during the transitions between glacial, interglacial, and interstadial periods. A logical beginning focus for First Americans research is on human response to global climatic change at the end of the last Ice Age. Fortunately, the late Asiatic Upper Paleolithic and late Ice Age American archaeological records provide unparalleled opportunities to examine human response to global environmental change—a topic of contemporary relevance.

2. To introduce new concepts and analytic techniques more consistent with the content and structure of the Late Pleistocene archaeological sites. One of the major weaknesses of First Americans research is the minimal amount of systematic survey carried out to search for Late Pleistocene settlement and land-use patterns. Most early human research in Asia and the Americas can be characterized as reactive, i.e., we react to the discovery of an interesting site or artifacts rather than systematically and proactively searching for such sites.

A major theme of First Americans research should be the investigation of variables, both environmental and demographic, that might have influenced hunter-gatherer groups' decisions concerning site placement and use, migration, and colonization. The archaeological record prior to the Clovis period, beginning at 11,500 years BP, remains painfully sparse. We still do not have a clear understanding of why these groups located sites where they did, much less where more early sites are likely to be found. We need to develop reliable procedures for isolating determinants of site location using empirical data.

3. To develop a chronological framework of well-dated archaeological and associated environmental remains based on radiometric dates (Kra 1988, 1989a, 1989b). Renee Kra's International Radiocarbon Data Base is an important pioneer effort to compile existing data and use a standardized protocol for evaluating radiocarbon dates. This world-wide compilation of radiocarbon dates can be queried to investigate a variety of topics by geographical area or by subject. It provides an important research tool for investigating Quaternary topics, including prehistoric archaeological sites and their environments.

An additional bright spot on the chronological front is the methodological advance represented by accelerator mass spectrometry (AMS). The AMS method provides a means for dating much smaller samples than was previously possible with conventional ^{14}C methods (Stafford 1991; Taylor 1991). With this new technology we now have a sufficiently precise technique to test numerous temporal hypotheses about migration, colonization, and adaptations to past environments.

4. To develop paleoenvironmental databases for the Late Pleistocene and Holocene periods. The formulation of local, regional, and global hypotheses relevant to First Americans studies requires synthesis and integration of information from a variety of disciplines. An incredible wealth of new information is now available (Ruddiman and Wright 1987). Computer technology coupled with database software provide a means for accessing relevant data from the allied disciplines of the Quaternary sciences. The advantages of the database approach are that it (1) imposes standards in recording data; (2) allows biases in existing data to be identified; and (3) permits massive volumes of data to be analyzed, displayed, and integrated. Electronic data storage provides the means for testing a wealth of hypotheses about cultural and environmental relationships on the local, regional, and global scales.

In a major ongoing effort, staff at the Illinois State Museum, Springfield, are developing publicly accessible databases to accommodate paleoecological information (Wiant and Graham 1987). *Paradox*, a standard relational database software, coupled with a Geographical Information System (GIS), accommodates both paleobotanical and faunal data. A paleobotanical *Database-North America and Europe* is being compiled with the ultimate objective of reconstructing paleoclimatic systems.

Entered variables include geology, ^{14}C dates, site location, and tree ring, historic, and oceanographic data. *FaunMap*, a database devoted to vertebrate remains from North America over the last 40,000 years, is a pilot project to compile systematically what is known about late Pleistocene and Holocene vertebrates in North America. Using an ARC/INFO program, digitized information can be plotted onto maps so that it is possible to examine the distribution of species by individuals or in communities in time series. The Minerals Management Service in the U.S. Department of the Interior has developed a computerized (in *dBASE IV*) *Archaeological and Shipwreck Information System* to provide information about submerged prehistoric sites on the U.S. continental shelf off the coasts of the lower forty-eight states.

5. To investigate the range and nature of archaeological site data, within each area, that will elucidate the various kinds of behavioral, organizational, and environmental patterns present. The Archeological Survey of Arkansas, with the support of the U.S. Army Corps of Engineers, has developed the database system *Automatic Manager of Archeological Site Data in Arkansas (AMASDA)*. This database, which covers the North American Southern Plains eight-state area, integrates with *GRASS*, a GIS relational database developed by the Corps of Engineers. A number of variables is included, such as remote sensing data, drainage, soils, geology, artificial boundaries, adaptation and bioarchaeological data, and report information about author and project. AMASDA bibliographical information is included within the National Park Service's computerized on-line *National Archeological Database (NADB)-Reports* of the grey (i.e., minimally reproduced and available) literature of U.S. archaeology (Canouts 1991). Numerous reports and overlay maps can be generated by this innovative system. The AMASDA system is now being applied to the U.S. Central and Northern Plains ten-state area by the Army Corps of Engineers (Ewen 1993). This system appears to be ideally suited for integrating data from a much larger area, and could be adapted to the task of integrating cultural and environmental data from Asia, North America, and South America important to understanding the peopling of the Americas.

6. To develop standardized classification and descriptive techniques for reporting artifacts. A brief glance at the artifact section of most site reports will attest to their scant and often inadequate descriptions. The lack of universally accepted terminology and different standards for reporting artifact formal dimensions, technology, use-wear, and raw materials used in artifact production have created a persistent problem. Poorly developed line drawings, weak supporting descriptions, and casual, inconsistent, and undescribed analytical procedures are among the many issues that now diminish the value of reports and make comparisons among archaeological assemblages difficult. These methodological issues must be addressed if we are to conduct credible science and generate meaningful reconstructions. As things now stand, scholars who are seriously interested in First Americans research must examine most collections first-hand by traveling to where collections are housed. This approach is extraordinarily expensive, time-consuming, and subjective.

Morlan (1991) has recommended the establishment of an international commission to develop a uniform terminology for archaeological artifact description. Standards can be most readily achieved by taking advantage of new advances in video and computer technology. It is now possible to store and manipulate artifact images in the computer; various image enhancement and morphometric techniques are now available in software packages that can be used to analyze computer images of artifacts and to measure dimensions and features of interest. The advantage of a visual digital imagery system is that artifact images from important sites can be stored in a database and electronically reproduced for use by many investigators. A prototype of this system is now in operation at the CSFA, and it appears to be a viable solution to the problem of comparing artifacts from distant parts of the world in greater detail than was previously possible. To maximize the benefits of this new technology, the commission's mandate should also include a directive to formulate standards for documenting images, develop a network to collect images, devise a protocol to regulate access to database information, and create a standardized nomenclature system.

In summary, to advance First Americans studies, the full array of disciplines and methods of modern science should be used to locate and investigate early sites and information. We must focus on developing quality site reports to provide the essential information for modeling migration and cultural development. Furthermore, the new technology of electronic data storage and processing promises to provide a framework for synthesizing a massive amount of multidisciplinary information. The flexibility offered by these databases will allow consideration of an almost infinite number of paleoecological and archaeological research questions. Database systems being developed in North America (radiocarbon, paleoecology, archaeology, bibliography, artifact imagery) must be integrated and expanded to include data from Asia and South America. Such an approach to the development of new knowledge in First Americans studies will allow numerous new questions to be considered as well as provide access to new data by a wider range of scholars than is now possible.

Biological Anthropology

Recently stimulated by the use of population differences in mitochondrial DNA to postulate the origin in Africa of modern humans between 200,000 and 100,000 years ago and their world-wide dispersal, research on the origins and dispersion of modern humans has become one of the most exciting and hotly debated issues in human natural history. International symposia have centered on the origin and dispersal of Asian populations (the University of Tokyo Symposium 1990), the peopling of the Pacific Rim (Krantz et al. 1989), and the biological affinities and origins of North American populations (*Human Biology* Vol. 64 [1992]).

There is resurgent scientific interest in the biological history of North American Indians (Armelagos et al. 1982, Harper and Laughlin 1982). During the first half of this century, interest in the biological and cultural histories of American Indians dominated North American archaeology. Frustration with the inability of this research to resolve intricate evolutionary history and biological relationships of American Indians resulted in most North American paleobiologists turning to more functional and ecological issues (Little 1982, Lovejoy et al. 1982, Meltzer 1983). Today, however, the biological history of indigenous North American populations as a part of the global population is becoming a major scholarship issue. Even a casual perusal of the current literature on the peopling of the New World documents that scholars are using a wide range of data to address the issues. For example, Turner (1989) bases his analyses on differences in the dentition of human populations, Szathmary (1989) uses genetic markers to evaluate phylogenetic relationships of peoples, Ossenberg (1989) analyzes nonmetrical cranial traits, Brace et al. (1989) rely on metrical analyses of the facial region and the dentition, and Howells (1973) and Steele and Powell (1992, 1994) rely on craniometric analyses that incorporate size and shape differences in the braincase as well as the face.

Although scholars differ in the data sets used to assess biological relationships and evolutionary histories, all recognize the necessity for large numbers of individuals to represent the populations being studied. We are one species, and differences between populations are of degree rather than of kind. Consequently, a population cannot be distinguished by the presence or absence of a single characteristic or even a few traits. Rather, populations are composed of individuals who tend to share common traits, and it is the frequency of these traits that distinguishes one population from another. Because traits are shared between populations, and it is their frequency that is distinctive, comparisons of large samples of many traits are necessary to assess accurately biological relationships between populations.

When extant populations are compared one to another, it is possible to establish a model or map of relative relationships of these living populations. To take the next step and infer from modern relationships the time that populations differentiated from one another requires scholars to accept major presumptions that have been difficult to verify. As examples, those models based upon living or near recent populations presume that rates of change are constant, that there has been no gene flow between populations after their initial divergence, and that all past populations are recognizable in the living populations.

Acknowledging these presumptions, it becomes evident that verification of these presumed relationships must be made, and that verification comes from the scholarly examination of our fossil record. When we evaluate the study of the fossil record of American human populations, however, we realize that the major emphasis has been on more recent populations, the peoples of the Late Prehistoric period. There have been several reasons for this focus. The most obvious reason is that adoption of agriculture allowed populations to increase in number, so there simply were more Late Prehistoric peoples and, therefore, more such sites to encounter. Secondly, archaeologists have been attracted to the major dwellings and community ruins left by these people, and, in the process of excavating these sites, have recovered relatively large samples of their biological remains. Another reason for the focus on more recent populations is that the older sites are more deeply buried, and thus difficult to locate and excavate. When older sites are encountered beneath more recent sites, time and resources have generally been expended to excavate the upper levels, so that the deeper earlier levels are little more than sampled. When scholars specifically seek early human sites, the terrain commonly has been altered so greatly over the years that it becomes difficult to predict their location. This is why so many of the early human sites have been found by serendipity and chance exposure.

Recognizing these problems, it becomes apparent that the archaeological and biological record of the earliest inhabitants of the Americas is limited and comes from widely dispersed localities. Compounding the issue further, the recovered individuals are represented by little in the way of physical remains. Typically, less than 20-25 percent of each Paleoindian skeleton has been preserved by nature. The consequence of all this is that many of America's early Holocene and late Pleistocene populations are represented by few bones from few sites. The verification of the relationships of living populations, the identification of extinct populations, and the understanding of the health and biological adaptations of these first Americans rests upon a very small, fragile, and irreplaceable sample.

It is in the area of First Americans bioanthropological research that American Indians and the archaeological/anthropological research community may find their strongest common ground.

First Americans bioanthropological study needs to follow these guidelines.

1. Make the best use of each sample of early modern humans available for study. Research on existing samples should be encouraged, casts should be made of all Paleoindian human skeletal material to facilitate this research, and the latest methods in computer-assisted data collection, imaging, and retrieval should be used. Further, meaningful consideration should be given by all parties on how to make the original remains available for future research that cannot be accommodated by analysis of previously recorded data, while treating those remains with the respect they deserve.

2. Fully investigate existing samples that may be of great antiquity. Until their antiquity can be verified, analysis of these remains lies in limbo.

3. Increase the efficiency of locating earlier sites. While the sensitive nature of actively seeking sites for the recovery of human remains is fully recognized, many of the earliest known sites have been disinterred by the erosive forces of nature and the human remains, once exposed, have soon deteriorated. Location of these sites would potentially significantly increase the sample of remains, as well as allow more effective monitoring of these sites against further damage.

4. Conduct research on furthering the accuracy of modeling biological relationships, based upon the evaluation of modern populations. These solutions will help to retrieve the most information from the limited American samples available for analysis.

Linguistics

Modern scientific linguistics is traditionally dated to the discovery by Sir William Jones of the genetic relationship between the classical languages of Europe, Latin and Greek, and the classical language of India, Sanskrit. In 1786 Jones announced in Calcutta his hypothesis that these languages must have "sprung from some common source, which, perhaps, no longer exists" (Lehman 1967). During the following century and a half, linguists proved the relationship and expanded the putative ancestral language family, now called *Indo-European* in English, to include most of the languages of Europe and many of those of western and south Asia as well. Classification of the languages was followed by eventually sophisticated attempts to reconstruct the Indo-European ancestor, based on comparison of their structures and vocabularies. The results were spectacular, in both their explanatory power and their provision of fruitful hypotheses for all of the human sciences, and nineteenth-century linguistics is rightly considered as one of the great scientific achievements of the period. Thus, from its very inception, and well into the present century, linguistics was regarded as a *historical* discipline, with pre-, proto-, and unrecorded history as its area of primary interest.

The rise of structural linguistics in the late 1920s shifted the interest of linguistic science to descriptive theory and language description, and concern with the historical implications of language study became less prominent. Since the 1950s, linguistics has been concerned mostly with the role of language in cognition, attempting to understand in particular how people learn and use languages.

Since the heyday of historical linguistics in the late nineteenth century, language as a tool for the study of prehistory has not, however, been neglected, and the abundance of sophisticated descriptive work produced in this century has made historical linguistics a powerful adjunct to the traditional historical sciences.

Work in language classification, with all that implies for prehistory, and the reconstruction of protolanguages, has been on the increase since its nadir in the 1950s and '60s, and present-day knowledge about deep relationships, theory and techniques of reconstruction, and the dynamics of diachronic change would astound our eighteenth- and nineteenth-century forebears.

Genetic classification of Amerindian languages—fraught with implications for the prehistory of the speakers of these languages—began almost as early as did concern about the provenience and prehistory of the better-known Old World languages. The labors of such scholars as Gallatin, Powell, Sapir, and Kroeber are too well known to require description here. Suffice it to say that there is at present no American language that has not been examined from the point of view of where it fits in the mosaic of American languages.

Early work on the American languages sought to establish family-level relationships, comparable to the principal branches of Indo-European such as Germanic or Slavic. Powell's (1891) work is a classic example of family-level classification. Later work sought to fit these low-level relationships into high-level categories comparable to Indo-Aryan within Indo-European, to Indo-European itself as a mother stock, or even higher constructs such as Nostratic, a super phylum including Indo-European and many other ancestral languages of western Asia. Sapir (1919), Swadesh (1959), and Greenberg (1987) are well-known examples of reductionist efforts of this kind.

Recently, however, most scholars of American languages have returned to splitting, based on much more stringent standards of proof of relationship (e.g., Campbell and Mithun 1979). Classification of South American languages, with a few notable exceptions, has always tended more to splitting than to lumping (cf. Loukotka 1968, Kaufman 1990).

Most of the early classificatory work, both chronologically and in terms of procedures used, involved inspection and suggestion of putative relationships on the basis of resemblances of form and meaning. Working hypotheses forged in this way were then subjected to detailed comparative work which sought to discover significant *systematic correspondences* between items. A large enough number of systematic correspondences permits a classification accepted by other scholars. The hypothesis has now become a theory.

Where the resemblances cannot be "proved" by recurrent correspondences of some kind, relationship is rejected. Obviously there is room for difference of opinion having to do with sufficiency of examples and standards of proof; Goddard and Campbell (1994) and Ruhlen (1994) are examples of such interpretative differences.

The "all or nothing" approach of the traditional comparative method works adequately when a relationship is close (there are always enough clear correspondences to permit throwing out those with problems) but less well as one goes back in time. At deep levels (anything beyond 6,000 years BP, although many would argue for even less time depth), resemblances are fewer and they cease to be tightly systematic. Many historical linguists stop probing at this point. But the resemblances (such as those called "Panamericanisms" by scholars of American languages) do not cease thereby to be intriguing and to demand some sort of explanation, even if not genetic.

Additional methodologies are needed, perhaps based on something other than the traditional iron-clad regularity required by the comparative method, which can deal with resemblances unamenable to standard techniques of comparison. It is very possible that a new approach will be directed at the global issue—not at the resemblances themselves, but at their very presence.

Statistics will certainly be one of the tools of such new methodologies, as will various kinds of typology. Arguments will of necessity be indirect and complex, but these facts should not and will not prevent the formulation of new techniques for addressing the multiplicity of language and other kinds of data now at hand.

One scholar of the native languages of the Americas, Johanna Nichols, is already moving in these directions, and her work is probably the most promising at the moment. In several recent papers (e.g., Nichols 1990, 1992), she uses primarily linguistic data to confront the question of when and how the Americas were settled. She assumes axiomatically that the peoplings of the Pacific Basin and the Americas were separate aspects of the same event. Solid dates for the earliest occupation of Australia and New Guinea establish a *terminus a quo*. Using much persuasive analogical argument, she fixes a date of settlement of the Americas somewhere between 40,000 and 50,000 years ago, corresponding with recent dates from Australia. Not surprisingly, Nichols's arguments draw on other disciplines as well (e.g., the history of agriculture for plant domestication), and her persuasive conclusions call into serious question the widely accepted Clovis-based chronology.

Work of this kind will make the picture of the settlement of the Americas clearer, and may well point toward conclusions even about linguistic prehistory which can not now be made on linguistic bases alone.

Regardless of shuffling and reshuffling by scholars, North and Central American languages are for the most part well documented and described; this corpus is in a state to be used indefinitely for scientific purposes. The same is not true of the languages of the southern American continent. Many languages have been lost there with scarcely a trace, and many others are on the verge of extinction, with little or no documentation. Rain forest species and languages are affected equally. Work on the documentation of the remaining native languages of South America must be an issue of highest priority for the study of American prehistory.

Conservation and Public Policy

Because of the multinational scope of First Americans resources and studies, no single institutional framework exists for the management (including the preservation, conservation, and use) of these resources. Indeed, no such framework exists within any nation whose lands hold archaeological and related paleoenvironmental materials relevant to First Americans research. This lack of a unified framework has impacted research and management policies and practices used to locate, investigate, and protect early sites and related data on public and private lands, and has led to a failure to make important research developments available through public education programs.

The focus of the symposium published in this volume was the public nature of the First Americans resource base, including the information derived from the archaeological and paleoenvironmental materials included in these resources. "There is a worldwide moral consensus that the long-term conservation of a significant portion of our cultural past is good for the human community" (Knudson 1984:245), and "all people . . . have stewardship responsibilities for . . . these resources . . . Ultimately, governments have archaeological stewardship responsibilities to act on the public's behalf" (Knudson, this volume). Former U.S. Secretary of the Interior Manuel Lujan, Jr. (1991) stated that "[the archeological paleoenvironmental record] is a public trust to be understood and evaluated to help shape our present responses to changing environments." This *public trust* concept and ethic are administered differently by various governments based primarily on (1) their legal heritage; and (2) the directness of each country's politically dominant population's ties with the culture represented by the archaeological remains within that country's administration. The legal heritage of Central and South American nations is directly tied to Roman or British common law. These nations generally have codified or regularly apply the public trust concept when dealing with heritage resources on all of their lands, whether those lands are privately or publicly owned. The legal basis in both the United States and Canada is also in British common and Roman law, but in addition both legal systems exhibit strong support for individual rights, developed in reaction to the traditional English power of the community (the government) over the individual (cf. Fowler, Knudson, this volume). Thus, the basic law or legal practice in these countries in most cases has asserted the priority of individual landowner rights over community heritage interests. How seriously and consistently any heritage protection codes are enforced also varies among nations, based in part on the economics of site looting and artifact trafficking as well as on the directness of the cultural ties of the enforcers and the threatened sites.

The authors of this paper are all based in North America, and those with public archaeological conservation or management experience are all U.S.-based. Thus, this discussion focuses on experiences in U.S. public archaeological conservation policies and practices. There is no national program for managing privately owned archaeological sites in the United States, but such programs operate through some state, tribal, and local governments. Elsewhere in this volume (Fowler, Magne, McGimsey) there are discussions of legal approaches to the protection of First Americans resources in other countries. However, none of these discussions addresses public resource management programs that can support, or sometimes inhibit or actually harm, First Americans research. The United States has an archaeological management program that must be applied on the 1.2 million square miles of federal U.S. public and Indian lands (a third of the nation). The following discussion of the implementation of U.S. public archaeological conservation policy is a basis for comparison of the public treatment of First Americans resources on both public and private lands inside and outside the United States as reflected in generic issues such as competing management interests, bureaucratic structures, and the conflict between scholarship and management (cf. Keel 1979, King 1987). Cleere (1989) has compiled an excellent set of papers on archaeological resource management around the world, with specific discussions of programs in the northern Andes, southern Ontario, Canada, and the former Union of Soviet Socialist Republics, as well as in the United States.

In addition to having a legal heritage oriented towards private rights, the dominant U.S. political and resource managerial community has few direct cultural ties to the prehistoric archaeology of First Americans resources. The U.S. National Trust for Historic Preservation was congressionally chartered in 1949 "to provide for the preservation of . . . antiquities of national significance . . . and to facilitate public participation in the preservation of sites, objects, and antiquities of national significance" (*Public Law* [P.L.] 408, 16 *United States Code* [U.S.C.] 461). The Trust has exhibited little interest in any prehistoric U.S. resources, much less those of the First Americans; however, that began to change in 1993 (Edmondson 1993). Historically, the Trust has apparently believed that archaeological resources are adequately addressed by the

Smithsonian Institution's National Museum of Natural History (note, not the National Museum of American History), which in the late nineteenth century encouraged the study of the First Americans as a bioevolutionary interest (Hinsley 1981:104-108). Similarly, academic disciplines generally differentiate among anthropology (including prehistoric archaeology), history or American Studies (often the home of historic archaeology), chemistry, physics, linguistics, geology, agricultural soils, and biology. Most people do not understand the complexities of First Americans research and resource management, which should be based on multidisciplinary analysis of nonhuman paleoenvironments as well as early prehistory and models of human genetics and language.

Given this perceptual background, it is no surprise that the U.S. legal framework for *in situ* management of First Americans resources is misunderstood. This legal framework only implicitly values the information content of U.S. archaeological sites, since it is oriented to protection in place. The U.S. Antiquities Act of 1906 made it a crime to disturb any prehistoric site on public lands without a permit, which was to be granted only to qualified individuals from recognized scientific or educational institutions, but the law does not include any explicit statement of why these sites are valuable. The intent of the law's scientific supporters was to reserve sites for scholarly research (Lee 1970), but codification of a monument preserve system in the same legislation was an expression of public recreational interests that frequently conflict with scientific analysis (Rothman 1989). The 1960 Reservoir Salvage Act (P.L. 86-523) was comparably phrased, as was its amendment ("Moss-Bennett," P.L. 93-291) in 1974. The latter included a mechanism to federally fund the recovery of "significant scientific, prehistorical, historical, or archeological data" if desired by the impacting federal agency or by the Secretary of the Interior. The Archaeological Resources Protection Act of 1979 (ARPA; P.L. 96-95) has a statement of findings and purpose that the law is to "secure, for the present and future benefit of the [United States] American people, the protection of archaeological resources and sites which are on public lands and Indian lands" (Sec. 2(b)), and this does not elaborate the scientific information values that are basic to the protected benefits.

In complement, the National Historic Preservation Act (NHPA) in 1966 stated that "the historical and cultural foundations of the Nation should be preserved . . . to give a sense of orientation to the American people" (P.L. 89-665, preamble) and included mechanisms for evaluating which heritage resources were important enough to preserve, and the appropriateness of such preservation in competition with economic developments (Sec. 106).

In the late 1960s the National Environmental Policy Act (NEPA; 42 *United States Code* [U.S.C.] 4321) stated that it was the "continuing responsibility of the Federal Government to . . . preserve important historic, cultural, and natural aspects of our national heritage [to enhance the quality of U.S. American life]" (Sec. 101(b)) and required publicly available documentation of resource management decisions. NEPA requires that interdisciplinary scientific analyses of resources and impacts to them be used in making those management decisions (Caldwell 1982). This policy statement does not mandate the protection of either archaeological material in place or its derived information values, but requires use of that information in decision making.

NEPA is a land use and resource legal tool that overrides the concept of private land ownership (Caldwell 1970, Knudson 1986:397-398), and has a scientific interdisciplinary basis that addresses both the natural and social world. There are comparable laws throughout the U.S. states, in Canada (Canadian Environmental Assessment Act of 1994, see Magne this volume) and its provinces and many nations, and several international lending institutions (e.g., World Bank) require environmental assessments as part of project funding approval. In the United States, NEPA clearly is an umbrella that includes all the resources of concern to First Americans studies. It is a planning tool, as are the U.S. state and Canadian provincial historic preservation plans and the resource management plans of the U.S. Forest Service, Bureau of Land Management, National Park Service, Army Corps of Engineers, and other agencies. Involvement of First Americans scholars in the development of these planning documents is a critical element in responsible stewardship of First Americans resources.

These archaeological, heritage, and environmental protection laws in the United States and other countries are all oriented to the public benefit and all include mechanisms that require rules, regulations, and regulatory bureaucracies keyed to funding cycles and personnel authorizations. None of the U.S. laws is explicitly focused on the research values of archaeological resources, though those are implicitly understood to be the basis for public understanding of the preserved heritage resources; the focus is on the protection of physical things first and information second. ARPA is most explicit about the protection of information and data, not just sites and objects. In these and other laws, *in situ* archaeological site protection has always been required to be conducted in a context of many land-based resources, all of which in turn have many uses.

First Americans scholars have had little involvement in the promulgation and implementation of this legislation. Most such scholars are in academia and museums, corporate cultures that have traditionally not encouraged public and political involvement by their members. Further, the individuals and organizations who develop legislation and the bureaucracy that implements it have their own culture, with which few First Americans scholars have had any familiarity or even interest. Yet that culture is responsible for the management of the publicly valued prehistoric First Americans resources and their included information, as a public trust.

Given this legal framework, how can First Americans scholars fulfill their world-wide public trust responsibilities to (1) identify American and related Asian archaeological and paleoenvironmental sites at least 10,000 years old; (2) conservatively derive their included information (Fowler 1986, Lipe 1974, Lujan 1991); and (3) conserve all or parts of them for future scholars and the interested public? A major basis for the answers to these questions lies in the research questions, methods, and techniques that were the focus of the conference reported in these volumes, and which are summarized in this chapter. A second important responsibility for scholars is to participate in public management and awareness activities that relate to First Americans resources.

In the United States, when the Moss-Bennett bill passed Congress in 1974, many archaeologists anticipated a future with increased research funding. They did not realize that the benefits of this legislation would not automatically be handed out to them in the form of expanded research funding. Instead, its distribution would be determined by a body of regulations formulated by individuals whose main interest was not necessarily the investigation of archaeological or other paleoenvironmental resources to gain maximum information. Archaeological resources on U.S. public lands are managed by agency land managers whose responsibilities are focused on their agency's congressionally mandated mission—which is generally anything but archaeological or paleoenvironmental protection or research (Keel 1979).

No U.S. laws protect noncultural paleoenvironmental data *per se*—including pollen, soils, tephra, plant and animal macrofossils, or landforms critical to First Americans research and public interpretation.

U.S. federal archaeology laws are generally place oriented, focused on the protective management of things in place, complemented by a concern for the management of objects removed from their original archaeological context. Therefore, inventory of those places that have protected archaeological resources is a priority for land-managing agencies, so that other uses can be authorized where no archaeological resources have been found. If publicly desirable economic developments cannot avoid important archaeological resources, time-consuming and expensive resource recovery is legally required. Thus, avoidance is desirable for both the land-managing agency and the land-using economic interest.

U.S. archaeological protection law only implicitly fosters desirable research (cf. Elston 1992). Most scholarly archaeologists in the United States did not understand the legal and bureaucratic frameworks developed to implement archaeological protection but, in order to conduct First Americans research on public lands, must now work within a system that has been constructed largely by bureaucratic non-scholars and non-archaeologists—and/or work toward changing the system.

Given the vast expanses of federal lands in the U.S. and numbers of projects requiring federal authorization and thus subject to NHPA, NEPA, or ARPA requirements, by the early 1970s a large number of archaeologists was required to conduct the mandated inventory, evaluation, and recovery of important archaeological resources. A similar situation developed in Canada. This led to the expansion of U. S. and Canadian public archaeology, including both government-employed and private contracting archaeologists. In the United States, the latter were required to have Antiquities Act, and subsequently ARPA, permits to conduct these archaeological investigations, but most such investigations required minimal technical or analytical archaeological training and provided few opportunities to conduct more synthetic studies. This compliance-oriented archaeological activity employed a lot of people, but did not produce much academically acceptable research—because its goals were quite different. The relatively complementary association of public and academic archaeology that had developed in the United States during the 1930s Works Progress Administration archaeological investigations, and which continued during the 1950s River Basin Surveys projects (Fowler 1986), rarely carried through in the 1970s and '80s public archaeology.

The growing separation of public and academic archaeology in North America in the late twentieth century has meant that academic contributions to theory, methods, and techniques used in public archaeological projects are usually secondhand. There has been significant dissension over who is a "professional" archaeologist, that appellation being more important to public archaeologists than it is to academicians defined by their affiliation. And there have been arguments about the nature of the resource when its regulatory status meant dollars to one person, while its research contribution meant more to another. Many words have been expended over the philosophical difference between the *significance* and *importance* of a North American archaeological site, from varying legal and scholarly perspectives. First Americans research is affected by all of this.

Archaeological resource management developed across the world over the last two decades. But in the United States, to protect all potentially useful information, every "cultural resource" (which includes archaeological as well as architectural and folklife resources [Knudson 1986]), however large or small, was sometimes identified as being every bit as important as any other cultural resource. The idea that key sites or sites of high integrity are of greater importance than a surface scatter of flakes was often denied, while at the same time undistinguished small sites of critical research value were identified as expendable. North American public compliance archaeology produces huge quantities of monograph-size publications outlining data-recovery plans, sample surveys, eligibility statements, memoranda of agreement, guidelines, rules and regulations, and innumerable other topics that are often judged to be irrelevant by scholarly archaeologists. These reports are written to meet regulatory requirements and guidelines, and often are almost unintelligible to anyone looking for information related to First Americans research. Most North American public archaeologists have little or no work time available for conducting synthetic analyses of the information acquired in compliance archaeology, much less the time and library necessary to publish scholarly treatises. The public's attitude is that research should be done in universities, and resource managers should manage; this is reflected in government agencies' lack of rewards for, or even authorization of, employee scholarship.

The minimally distributed "grey literature" of North American public archaeology includes important information about where sites have and have not been found, and sometimes important clues to First Americans archaeological and paleoenvironmental resource locations and characteristics, but worthwhile data are difficult to extract and have not been abstracted. As a result, anyone wishing to do research with this literature must spend innumerable hours separating out valuable data from legally required documentation of data and processes. As mentioned earlier, a *National Archaeological Database (NADB)-Reports*, a computerized bibliography of reports and other written products of U.S. archaeological investigations, is being developed (Canouts 1991) and in 1994 included more than 150,000 citations. Keyword categories are to be included in the future. Inclusion within *NADB-Reports* of keywords significant to First Americans research is important. This system is available on-line and the U.S. National Park Service, which has developed several *NADB* modules, is presently talking with other countries about linking systems to create international archaeological bibliographies.

Probably over 90 percent of the archaeological sites known to occur in the United States and Canada have been identified during compliance archaeology, and their publicly available documentation is rarely found anywhere but in the grey literature. While most of the well-known First Americans sites have been found by amateurs (Knudson 1991), they are few in number compared with the information collected by public archaeology projects. Many critical First Americans resources are currently identified only in compliance inventory records. The relative inaccessibility of important First Americans resource identification information is aggravated by the refusal of the U.S. National Science Foundation (NSF) to support baseline archaeological site inventory, believing that such information should be provided in other ways (by the land-managing agency compliance inventory?) to identify sites important enough for NSF support of their analytical investigation.

Many conflicts of interest have surfaced in North American public archaeology, all of which affect First Americans research and most of which are reflected in other nations' public archaeology programs. In the United States, the same agencies that issue archaeological permits often judge the results of the permitted work in reviewing related land management decisions. Research is encouraged, in most circumstances, only with non-agency funds unless there has been agency support through a development project, which tends to result in site destruction through "mitigative" excavation and analyses (see Douglas, this volume). Like archaeological investigations related to land management, exploitation of an archaeological resource on U.S. public land must be done under a permit even when the only goal is the aquisition of information through proper scientific query. All such land-use permits—which have been required for archeological work on public lands in the

United States since 1906—must be justified as being in the public interest. In the 1990s, U.S. public land is managed under a complex web of overlapping and sometimes competing laws, regulations, and guidelines. Because these laws are directed to site *protection* or *preservation*, and because archaeological excavation is inherently destructive of a nonrenewable site, it can be legally difficult for a U.S. public archaeologist to justify to resource managers—who are not archaeologists, but are empowered to issue the permits—the excavation and study of an otherwise unthreatened archaeological resource.

Some public archaeologists bring superior research credentials to their contracts and jobs, but many have only minimal academic backgrounds and have very nontechnical, bureaucratic responsibilities that however include critical recommendations about resource values and research authorities. Many of these individuals are over-committed members of under-staffed agencies, which in turn are compliance driven within a very complex bureaucracy.

To reestablish the traditional link between scholarly and public archaeology, to support the study as well as the conservation of First Americans resources, the following measures are proposed.

1. Every practicing First Americans scholar should develop a working knowledge of the land-based resource laws, regulations, guidelines, and managing agencies that impinge on First Americans research in that scholar's country and research area. Participation in broad environmental assessment and management activities is desirable, to find out how to locate key First Americans data in the masses of paper and jargon that go with multi-resource environmental management documentation. A critical element in First Americans resource conservation is to learn about any available regional historic preservation plans (e.g., an excellent planning document just for Paleoindian resources in Georgia in the United States [Anderson et al. 1990]) and other land use plans.

2. Within each country holding First Americans resources, the national science academy should evaluate the relationship

between First Americans scholarly research and public man-agement of First Americans resources, and recommend any needed public program and policy changes to enhance re-search in the public interest. It is appropriate that such an oversight review be conducted at a national level, involving individuals knowledgeable about the country's resource man-agement needs and current programs, about multidisciplinary First Americans research needs, and about specific field and analytical/curatorial archaeological conservation methods and techniques.

3. Every post-secondary archaeology education program should provide courses on topics such as archaeology and the law, archaeological research and conservation, archaeological project fiscal and personnel administration, and ethics and archaeology. Discussions of laws and programs affecting noncultural paleoenvironmental Holocene and Late Pleisto-cene data critical to First Americans research should be included.

4. Every graduate archaeology program should include a minimum course requirement in heritage resource manage-ment and relevant local, state, provincial, tribal, national, and international legislation, and in general environmental man-agement. Environmental management education should address specialized programs such as air, water, endangered species, and wetlands conservation, where they exist, because of the potential effects of those management programs on multidisciplinary First Americans resources.

5. Public resource management agencies and resource development organizations that encounter First Americans resources should support scholarly research related to those resources, not just minimal identification, evaluation, and avoidance. Completion of research on rare and nonrenewable First Americans archaeological and paleoenvironmental resources is in the public interest (e.g., in relation to understanding global climatic change), providing information for public education and recreation as well as for more reliable evaluations of the management needs of other First Americans resources encountered in the future.

6. Organizations developing broad bibliographic or resource description databases should include keywords or other information identifiers that relate to First Americans research. This is particularly important in the U.S. National Park Service's development of *NADB-Reports* keywords, since that program could become an international model.

7. Professional and avocational archaeological organizations should be encouraged to establish and maintain forums for the two-way exchange of information between academic and public archaeologists, and from these should come programs to oversee and advise government archaeological resource management programs. This should involve more active participation in the development of laws, regulations, policies, and guidelines, at every governmental level.

8. First Americans scholars should encourage the professional and public organizations of which they are members to reward public servants for good management of First Americans resources. Such rewards should be for non-archaeologists as well as archaeologists who protect the cultural and paleoenvironmental information so critical to First Americans studies.

9. First Americans scholars should participate in the development of general land/resource management planning documents, and should be involved by planning agencies from the earliest planning stages through project decision-making and implementation. Agencies should routinely involve prehistory scholars with paleoenvironment research experience, usually found outside the agency, at a local college or museum, in all major planning efforts. Such expertise can often be critical in identifying project opportunities or constraints as early as possible in the planning effort. For scholars, this begins with finding out what planning documents are being written or scheduled in their home region or region of research interest, and identifying critical concerns to the agency. It involves understanding the decision-making process and the agency's mission and responsibilities, careful reading of the draft plans, and providing useful and timely review comments to the management agency. If individual scholars do not have the time or interest in being so involved, they should ensure that someone else with First Americans research interests is involved in such planning efforts.

First Americans Studies in a Public Arena

Stewardship of humanity's past constitutes a challenge of immense proportions. Largely through the efforts of a dedicated few, the scope of the challenge is becoming more clearly defined. Traditionally the responsibility for preserving and conserving our cultural heritage has fallen on the archaeological profession. It is now apparent that, for those professionals as well as for the nonprofessional archaeological public, responsible stewardship has diverse implications that include social, political, legal, educational, economic (e.g., land development, pollution control, tourism), and other dimensions.

There is a need for immediate collaboration among cultural, natural, and geophysical scholars, economists, and constitutional law experts to formulate strategies and policies for the conservation and preservation of First Americans resources on private and public lands in all countries. One of the greatest imperatives facing individuals and groups interested in our earliest cultural heritage is the need to identify the key players in heritage preservation and to legitimize their roles and responsibilities within a voluntary association of dedicated participants sharing common concerns, goals, and objectives.

We also need coordinating mechanisms at the local, national, and international levels, greater public awareness and understanding of heritage issues through mass media and public education, and to move heritage conservation from the periphery to the mainstream of public life and consciousness. Although state, provincial, tribal, national, and United Nations agencies do exist that have been charged with the responsibility of conserving humanity's cultural and biological heritage, coordination of efforts in the past can be characterized as generally ad hoc and crisis oriented. It is imperative that protocols be established, taking advantage of breakthroughs in information technology, to facilitate dissemination of information relating to First Americans heritage preservation. In this era of international cooperation among once-rival nations, the opportunity exists to forge links among institutions and individuals who share an interest and commitment to preserving humanity's past and the record of the First Americans.

Public outreach and education have never been more vital than at present to inculcate a concern for heritage preservation and concern. Celebrities such as Jean Auel, author of *The Clan of the Cave Bear* and several other well-researched "Paleolithic romances," have had an extraordinarily positive effect on shaping public perceptions of the human past. In turn, Auel (1991:125) has noted: "If the scientist wants the cooperation of the public, it is the responsibility of the scientist to communicate in ways that are understandable."

School educators and curriculum planners need to be recruited into the process of enhancing public awareness of First Americans heritage issues and environmental values, so that American citizens do not continue to regard the hemisphere's cultural heritage as an expendable commodity that represents only an alien culture and benefits only a privileged few.

An important element in all First Americans scholarship should be the involvement of today's American Indians in the investigation of their own heritage and its resources. Information should be developed for American Indian heritage programs, and American Indians should be trained (with financial support) and employed in First Americans studies. That is part of the responsibility of using as well as conserving such an important element of the public archaeological trust as First Americans resources.

The First World Summit Conference on the Peopling of the Americas afforded an unparalleled opportunity to convene some of the leading players in heritage conservation and to provide a forum for discussing goals in managing First Americans resources to support scholarly research that in turn supports public understanding of the past. Issues raised at Summit '89 point to topics seriously in need of public debate. How can the current approach to heritage research, conservation, education, and recreation be modified to benefit First

Americans resources? How can the public's awareness, understanding, and appreciation of First Americans heritage issues be achieved at all sociopolitical levels? What steps can be taken to increase communication and cooperation among the various cultural and natural resource private and public sector organizations, to benefit First Americans resources? What can be done to achieve optimal division of heritage management responsibilities among private and public individuals and sectors to foster global cooperation on First Americans heritage issues of mutual concern? What measures can be taken to ensure adequate funding for meritorious First Americans research, conservation, and public education projects?

Conclusion

Scientific research drives what is known about First Americans studies and provides the basic information on which conservation and education programs should be based. We need to locate First Americans resources, and then to develop high-quality site reports using the full complement of methods and concepts offered by the Quaternary sciences and contemporary archaeology. Local site and environmental information can be integrated into an international database focusing on First Americans studies. This information is of interest to the research community and the public, and its value can be communicated to those resource managers charged with stewardship responsibilities. Participation in the public forums that affect the implementation of the First Americans public trust is a critical responsibility for the scholarly community.

Conservation policy is incomplete and First Americans cultural resources are inadequately protected. To focus research, protect First Americans resources, and educate the public and school children about America's earliest cultural heritage, leadership is needed to coordinate the efforts of all nations, organizations, and individuals involved in this important public program.

References Cited

Agenbroad, L.D., J.I. Mead, and L.W. Nelson (editors)
1990 *Megafauna & Man: Discovery of America's Heartland*. The
    Mammoth Site of Hot Springs, South Dakota, Inc., Scientific
    Papers, Volume 1, Hot Springs.

Anderson, D.G., R.J. Ledbetter, and L. O'Steen
1990 Paleoindian Period Archaeology of Georgia. *University of
    Georgia Laboratory of Archaeology Series Report* No. 28; *Georgia
    Archaeological Research Design Paper* No. 6.

Armelagos, G.J., D.S. Carlson, and D.P. Van-Gerven
1982 The Theoretical Foundations and Development of Skeletal
    Biology. In *A History of American Physical Anthropology
    1930-1980*, edited by F. Spencer, pp. 305-328. Academic Press,
    New York.

Auel, Jean M.
1991 Romancing the Public. In *Protecting the Past*, edited by G.S.
    Smith and J.E. Ehrenhard, pp. 123-127. CRC Press, Inc., Boca
    Raton, Florida.

Bonnichsen, R., and M.H. Sorg (editors)
1989 *Bone Modification*. Center for the Study of the First Americans,
    University of Maine, Orono.

Bonnichsen, R., and K. Turnmire (editors)
1991 *Clovis: Origins and Adaptations*. Center for the Study of the First
    Americans, Oregon State University, Corvallis.

Bonnichsen, R., and D.G. Steele (editors)
1994 *Method and Theory for Investigating the Peopling of the Americas*.
    Center for the Study of the First Americans, Oregon State
    University, Corvallis.

Bonnichsen, R., J. Tomenchuk, and F. Ikawa-Smith (editors)
Forthcoming (a). *Ice Age Archaeology of Asia*. Center for the Study of
    the First Americans, Oregon State University, Corvallis.

Bonnichsen, R., G.C. Frison, and K. Turnmire (editors)
Forthcoming (b). *Ice Age Peoples of North America*. Center for the
    Study of the First Americans, Oregon State University, Corvallis.

Bonnichsen, R., and T. Dillehay (editors)
Forthcoming. *Ice Age Peoples of Central and South America*. Center for
    the Study of the First Americans, Oregon State University,
    Corvallis.

Brace, C.L., Li Youngji, K.D. Hunt, Zhang Zhenbiao, and M.L. Brace
1989 A Cranio-facial Comparison of Circum-Pacific Peoples. In *Circum-Pacific Prehistory Conference, August 1-6, 1989, Reprint Proceedings* No. 1, edited by G. Krantz, Ho Chuan Kun, and M. Stoneking. Washington Centennial Pacific Celebration, Seattle.

Broeker, W.S., and G.H. Denton
1990a The Role of Ocean-atmosphere Reorganizations in Glacial Cycles. *Geochimica et Cosmochimica Acta* 53:2465-2501.

1990b What Drives Glacial Cycles? *Scientific American* 262:48-56.

Bryan, A.L. (editor)
1986 *New Evidence for the Pleistocene Peopling of the Americas*. Center for the Study of Early Man, University of Maine, Orono.

1991 The Fluted Point Tradition in the Americas—One of Several Adaptations to Late Pleistocene American Environments. In *Clovis: Origins and Adaptations*, edited by R. Bonnichsen and K. Turnmire, pp. 15-33. Center for the Study of the First Americans, Oregon State University, Corvallis.

Caldwell, L.K.
1970 An Ecosystems Approach to Public Land Policy. In *Public Land Policy: Proceedings of the Western Resources Conference held at Fort Collins, CO, 1968*, edited by P.O. Foss, pp. 43-56. Associated University Press, Boulder, Colorado.

1982 *Science and the National Environmental Policy Act*. The University of Alabama Press, University.

Campbell, L., and M. Mithun (editors)
1979 *The Languages of Native America: Historical and Comparative Assessment*. University of Texas Press, Austin.

Canouts, V.
1991 Computerized Information Exchange on the Local and National Levels. *Sites & Monuments: National Archaeological Records*, edited by C.U. Larsen, pp. 231-247. The National Museum of Denmark, Copenhagen.

Carlisle, R.C. (editor)
1988 *Americans Before Columbus: Ice-Age Origins*. Ethnology Monographs No. 12. Department of Anthropology, University of Pittsburgh, Pittsburgh, Pennsylvania.

Clark, D.W.
1991 The Northern (Alaska-Yukon) Fluted Points. In *Clovis: Origins and Adaptations*, edited by R. Bonnichsen and K. Turnmire, pp. 35-48. Center for the Study of the First Americans, Oregon State University, Corvallis.

Cleere, H.F. (editor)
1989 *Archaeological Heritage Management in the Modern World*. Unwin Hyman, London.

Dillehay, T.D., G. Ardila C., G. Beltrao, and G. Politis
1992 Earliest Hunters and Gatherers of South America. *Journal of World Prehistory* 6(2):145-204.

Dillehay, T.D., and D.J. Meltzer (editors)
1991 *The First Americans: Searvch and Research.* CRC Press, Inc., Boca Raton, Florida.

Edmondson, P.
1993 National Trust Involvement with Archaeological Issues: A Summary. Ms. presented to the National Trust Archaeology Task Force, November 15, 1993; on file, National Trust for Historic Preservation, Washington.

Elston, R.G.
1992 Archaeological Research in the Context of Cultural Resource Management: Pushing Back in the 1990s. *Journal of California and Great Basin Anthropology* 14(1):37-48.

Ewen, C.R.
1993 An Archeological Legacy: Central and Northern Great Plains Overview. *Federal Archeology* 6(1):7.

Fowler, D.D.
1986 Conserving American Archaeological Resources. In *American Archaeology Past and Future*, edited by D.J. Meltzer, D.D. Fowler, and J.A. Sabloff, pp. 135-162. Smithsonian Institution Press, Washington.

Frison, G.C.
1991 The Goshen Cultural Complex: New Data for Paleoindian Research. In *Clovis: Origins and Adaptations*, edited by R. Bonnichsen and K. Turnmire, pp. 133-151. The Center for the Study of the First Americans, Oregon State University, Corvallis.

Goddard, I., and L. Campbell
1994. The History and Classification of American Indian Languages: What Are the Implications for the Peopling of the Americas? In *Method and Theory for Investigating the Peopling of the Americas*, edited by R. Bonnichsen and D.G. Steele. Center for the Study of the First Americans, Oregon State University, Corvallis.

Goebel, F.E., W.R. Powers, and N.H. Bigelow
1991 The Nenana Complex of Alaska and Clovis Origins. In *Clovis: Origins and Adaptations*, edited by R. Bonnichsen and K. Turnmire, pp. 49-79. Center for the Study of the First Americans, Oregon State University, Corvallis.

Greenberg, J.H.
1987 *Language in the Americas*. Stanford University Press, Palo Alto, California.

Gruhn, R.
1991 Stratified Radiocarbon Dated Archaeological Sites of Clovis Age and Older in Brazil. In *Clovis: Origins and Adaptations*, edited by R. Bonnichsen and K. Turnmire, pp. 283-286. Center for the Study of the First Americans, Oregon State University, Corvallis.

Harper, A.B., and W.S. Laughlin
1982 Inquiries Into the Peopling of the New World: Development of Ideas and Recent Advances. In *A History of American Physical Anthropology 1930-1980*, edited by F. Spencer, pp. 281-304. Academic Press, New York.

Hinsley, C.M., Jr.
1981 *Savages and Scientists. The Smithsonian Institution and the Development of American Anthropology 1846-1910*. Smithsonian Institution Press, Washington.

Howells, W.W.
1973 Cranial Variation in Man: A Study by Multivariate Analysis of Patterns of Difference Among Recent Human Populations. *Papers of the Peabody Museum of Archaeology and Ethnology, Harvard University*, Volume 67.

Kaufman, T.
1990 Language History in South America: What We know and How to Know More. *Amazonian Linguistics: Studies in Lowland South American Languages*, edited by D. Payne, pp. 13-73. University of Texas Press, Austin.

Keel, B.C.
1979 A View from Inside. *American Antiquity* 44:164-170.

King, T.F.
1987 Prehistory and Beyond: The Place of Archaeology. In *The American Mosaic: Preserving a Nation's Heritage*, edited by R.E. Stipe and A.J. Lee, pp. 235-264. U.S. Committee, International Council on Monuments and Sites, Washington.

Knudson, R.
1984 Ethical Decision Making and Participation in the Politics of Archaeology. In *Ethics and Values in Archaeology*, edited by E.L. Green, pp. 243-264. The Free Press, Collier-Macmillan, New York.

1986 Contemporary Cultural Resource Management. In *American Archaeology Past and Future*, edited by D.J. Meltzer, D.D. Fowler, and J.A. Sabloff, pp. 395-413. Smithsonian Institution Press, Washington.

1991 Paleoindian Paradigms. Presentation in the Symposium on Paleoindian-Upper Paleolithic Relations, June 13-15, Denver, Colorado.

Kra, R.
1988 Updating the Past: The Establishment of the International Radiocarbon Data Base. *American Antiquity* 53:118-125.

1989a The International Radiocarbon Data Base: A Progress Report. *Radiocarbon* 31:1067-1076.

1989b Report of the International Radiocarbon Database Workshop. *Radiocarbon* 31:1080-1082.

Krantz, G., Ho Chuan Kun, and M. Stoneking (organizers)
1989 *Circum-Pacific Prehistory Conference, August 1-6, 1989, Reprint Proceedings*. Washington Centennial Pacific Celebration, Seattle.

Lee, R.F.
1970 *The Antiquities Act of 1906*. U.S. Department of the Interior, National Park Service, Washington.

Lehmann, W.P.
1967 *A Reader in Nineteenth-Century Historical Indo-European Linguistics*. Indiana University Press, Bloomington, Indiana.

Lipe, W.D.
1974 A Conservation Model for American Archaeology. *Kiva* 39:213-245.

Little, M.
1982 The Development of Ideas About Humans Ecology and Adaptation. In *A History of American Physical Anthropology 1930-1980*, edited by F. Spencer, pp. 405-434. Academic Press, New York.

Loukotka, C.
1968 *Classification of South American Indian Languages*, edited by J. Wilbert. Latin American Center, University of California, Los Angeles.

Lovejoy, C.O., R.P. Mensforth, and G.J. Armelagos
1982 Five Decades of Skeletal Biology as Reflected in the American
     Journal of Physical Anthropology. In *A History of American
     Physical Anthropology 1930-1980*, edited by F. Spencer, pp.
     329-337. Academic Press, New York.

Lujan, M., Jr.
1991 *A National Strategy for Federal Archeology*. Papers of the U.S.
     Secretary of the Interior, October 24, 1991.

Mead, J.I., and D.J. Meltzer (editors)
1985 *Environments and Extinctions: Man in Late Glacial North America*.
     Center for the Study of Early Man, University of Maine, Orono.

Meltzer, D.J.
1983 The Antiquity of Man and the Development of American
     Archaeology. In *Advances in Archaeological Method and Theory* vol.
     6, edited by M.B. Schiffer, pp. 1-51. Academic Press, New York.

Morlan, R.E.
1991 Peopling of the New World: A Discussion. In *Clovis: Origins
     and Adaptations*, edited by R. Bonnichsen and K. Turnmire, pp.
     303-307. Center for the Study of the First Americans, Oregon
     State University, Corvallis.

Nichols, J.
1990 Linguistic Diversity and the First Settlement of the New
     World. *Language* 66(3):475-521.

1992 *Linguistic Diversity in Time and Space*. University of Chicago
     Press.

Nunez, L., and B. Meggers
1987 *Estudios Atacamenos: Investigaciones Paleoindio al Sur de la Linea
     Ecuatorial*. Universidad del Norte, Instituto de Investigaciones
     Arqueologicas R. P. Gustavo Le Paige, S.J., San Pedro de
     Atacama (II Region). Chile.

Ossenberg, N.S.
1989 Nonmetric Traits of the Skull Reveal Affinities Between
     People of Northeast Asia and Northwest North American. In
     *Circum-Pacific Prehistory Conference, August 1-6, 1989:,Reprint
     Proceedings* No. 1, edited by G. Krantz, Ho Chuan Kun, and M.
     Stoneking. Washington Centennial Pacific Celebration, Seattle.

Politis, G.
1991 Fishtail Projectile Points in the Southern Cone of South
     America: An Overview. In *Clovis: Origins and Adaptations*, edited
     by R. Bonnichsen and K. Turnmire, pp. 287-301. Center for the
     Study of the First Americans, Oregon State University, Corvallis.

Powell, J.W.
1891 Indian Linguistic Families of America North of Mexico. *Seventh Annual Report of the Bureau of American Ethnology of the Smithsonian Institution*, pp. 1-142. U.S. Government Printing Office, Washington.

Rothman, H.
1989 *Preserving Different Pasts*. University of Illinois Press, Urbana.

Ruddiman, W.F., and H.E. Wright, Jr. (editors)
1987 *North America and Adjacent Oceans During the Last Glaciation*. DYNAG volume K-3. Geological Society of North America, Boulder, Colorado.

Ruhlen, M.
1994. Linguistic Evidence for the Peopling of the Americas. In *Method and Theory for Investigating the Peopling of the Americas*, edited by R. Bonnichsen and D.G. Steele. Center for the Study of the First Americans, Oregon State University, Corvallis.

Sapir, E.
1919 Central and North American Languages. In *Encyclopaedia Brittanica*, 14th ed., 5:138-141.

Stafford, T.W.
1994. Accelerator C-14 Dating of Human Fossil Skeletons: Assessing Measurement Accuracy and Experimental Results. In *Method and Theory for Investigating the Peopling of the Americas*, edited by R. Bonnichsen and D.G. Steele. Center for the Study of the First Americans, Oregon State University, Corvallis.

Stanford, D.J., and J. Day (editors)
1991 *Ice Age Hunters of the Rockies*. University of Colorado Press, Boulder.

Steele, D.G., and J.F. Powell
1992 Peopling of the Americas: Paleobiological Evidence. *Human Biology* 64:303-336.
1994 Paleobiological Evidence of the Peopling of the Americas: A Morphometric View. In *Method and Theory for the Peopling of the Americas*, edited by R. Bonnichsen and D.G. Steele. Oregon State University Press, Corvallis.

Swadesh, M.
1959 *Mapas de Clasificacion Linguistica de Mexico y las Americas*. Universidad Nacional Autonoma de Mexico, Mexico City.

Szathmary, E.J.E.
1989 Modeling Ancient Population Relationships from Modern
    Population Genetics. In *Abstracts: The First World Summit
    Conference of the Peopling of the Americas*, edited by J. Tomenchuk
    and R. Bonnichsen, p. 16. Center for the Study of the First
    Americans, University of Maine, Orono.

Tankersley, K.B., and B.L. Isaac (editors)
1990 *Early Paleoindian Economies of Eastern North America*. Research
    in Economic Anthropology: Supplement 5. JAI Press,
    Greenwich, Connecticut.

Taylor, R.E.
1994. Radiocarbon Dating of Bone by Accelerator Mass
    Spectrometry: Current Discussions and Future Directions. In
    Method and Theory for Investigating the Peopling of the Americas,
    edited by R. Bonnichsen and D.G. Steele. Center for the Study of
    the First Americans, Oregon State University, Corvallis.

Turner, C.G.
1989 Out of Southeast Asia: Dentition and the Peopling of the
    Pacific Basin and Adjoining Areas. In *Circum-Pacific Prehistory
    Conference, August 1-6, 1989, Reprint Proceedings No. 1*, edited by
    G. Krantz, Ho Chuan Kun, and M. Stoneking. Washington
    Centennial Pacific Celebration, Seattle.

The University of Tokyo Symposium
1990 *The Evolution and Dispersal of Modern Humans in Asia. November
    14-17, 1990: Abstracts*. The University Museum, The University
    of Tokyo, Japan.

Wiant, M.D., and R.W. Graham
1987 Mapping Illinois' Cultural and Paleobiological Resources.
    *Proceedings, 1987 National Symposium on Mining Hydrology,
    Sedimentology, and Reclamation*, pp. 27-29. University of
    Kentucky, Lexington.

IV. The Legal Environment

Archaeology, like most other human endeavors, is controlled to one degree or another by legal constraints. For example, how and where archaeological excavations take place may be controlled by property rights, both private and public. All things being equal, an archaeologist, unless he or she is the title holder personally, must have the consent of a landowner before conducting excavations. Even if the property is owned by the archaeologist, other legal requirements may impact the conduct of the work. In the United States, if the resource is owned by the government, permits must be obtained from the appropriate land-managing agency, be it local, state, or federal property or tribal trust land. In the United States and Australia, archaeologists may be legally impeded by state or higher jurisdictional requirements from conducting excavations at sacred or mortuary sites.

In many parts of the world the legal environment of archaeology is changing, with increased opposition from native peoples to archaeological impacts on their religious rights, supported by national as well as international publics. All archaeologists decry the destruction of archaeological resources by vandalism, but often find themselves viewed as vandals by native people. As a group that sees itself conducting its business for the enrichment of all citizens, archaeologists are disturbed by the outcry of native people and are in the process of adjusting their professional values and culture in response.

Archaeologists have made tremendous strides in protecting the prehistoric and historic cultural heritage by lobbying efforts with local, state, national, and international legislative bodies. Raising public money for archaeological data recovery and resource inventories has been successful in some countries. These successful legislative efforts must certainly be the result of public awareness that the cultural heritage manifested in the archaeological record is a valuable national commodity. Each government has a responsibility to afford some control over its consumption.

The following papers explore some of the legal environments in which First Americans scholars conduct their work. As the papers point out, most of the laws discussed here are protective in intent and reactive in their implementation. Most of the cited laws seek to protect national heritages, restrict access to archaeological properties, control the ownership of archaeological specimens, and govern their export from the country of origin. Additionally, legal systems such as those in Canada and the United States at least require bureaucratic consideration of the impact of development on public or privately owned resources directly or indirectly affected by governmental actions. Despite the particular perspective from which the individual nations view their archaeological heritage, their legislative efforts presume the national importance of humankind's past and its arts and monuments.

Bennie C. Keel
Ruthann Knudson

The Legal Structure for the Protection of Archaeological Resources in the United States and Canada

John M. Fowler

The English common-law tradition is basic to much United States and Canadian law, and over the past several decades both nations have responded to similar threats to prehistoric and historic resources. Both nations have given attention to the rights and interests of Native Americans in those resources. The National Historic Preservation Act as amended is the keystone to U.S. federal historic preservation law, which relies heavily on the National Register of Historic Places and the "Section 106" consultation process to deter damage to significant historic properties. Each of the U.S. states and territories and the District of Columbia have their own preservation law, and these are complemented by many local preservation requirements. Private law approaches to preservation (e.g., easements, zoning restrictions) are being used increasingly in both the United States and Canada. Canada's lack of a strong federal preservation mandate has resulted in placement of stronger preservation emphasis on the provincial levels.

The legal systems of the United States and Canada are strongly rooted in the English common-law tradition. Likewise, they share the federal form of government, which lodges certain powers with the national government and reserves others to state or provincial and local authorities. As a result, while the U.S. and Canadian programs for protecting and managing cultural resources are hardly identical, they do share many similar mechanisms and concepts. This paper will provide an overview of the U.S. legal structure for protecting archaeological resources and then briefly compare the Canadian experience.

As the national preservation programs have evolved over the past three decades, both countries have responded to similar threats to historic properties. The expansion of urban centers, development of transportation systems, and exploitation of energy resources have wreaked havoc on historic structures and archaeological resources in both countries. In turn, this has led to the enactment of new laws at the national, tribal, state/provincial, and local levels of government, supplementing existing authorities that had afforded more limited protection.

Historically, the development of preservation laws in both countries has been reactive to the immediate threats of the time. Thus, in the United States, for example, early legal responses focused on the looting of prehistoric archaeological sites in the Southwest. Later recognition of the importance of historic structures and districts led to further legal enactments. The Canadian experience has not been dissimilar. An important consequence is that a distinct body of law has evolved in both countries regarding the protection of archaeological resources, with provisions uniquely applicable to those properties and often somewhat apart from broader historic preservation laws and programs.

Likewise, there recently has been much attention given to the rights and interests of Native Americans in those items and human remains that not only possess archaeological or historic value but also have important associations with cultural traditions and religious beliefs. This has fostered an ongoing debate regarding the tension between scientific investigation and the sanctity of human remains and grave goods. Recent U.S. law on this issue will be discussed below.

The U.S. National Historic Preservation Program

The structure of preservation law in the United States is determined largely by the principles of federalism and the traditional allocation of legal authority and political power to the various levels of government. As a result, while a cohesive program of administrative structures and legal protections exists at the national government level, the most stringent protections are provided for historic properties at the local level, the traditional repository of authority over land use. Indeed, it is important to note that no provision of federal law exists to prohibit the destruction of a historic resource, unless it is in federal ownership.

Federal Programs and Protections

At the outset, a distinction must be drawn between federal laws that apply to federal and to nonfederal lands. Not surprisingly, the most stringent U.S. protections for archaeological and historic properties apply only to those properties in government ownership. It is also important to note that the broad provisions of laws concerning all kinds of historic properties are augmented by several federal laws that are designed specifically for the protection of archaeological resources.

The National Environmental Policy Act of 1969 (42 USC [*U.S. Code*] 4321, 4331, 4332) declared that it was national policy to "assure for all Americans . . . culturally pleasing surroundings" and to "preserve important historic, cultural . . . aspects of our national heritage." This broad provision has resulted in consideration of archaeological (including First Americans) sites threatened by development activities across the United States, but offers no legal protection per se.

The keystone of federal historic preservation law is the National Historic Preservation Act of 1966 (NHPA; 16 USC 470) as amended. It establishes the basic elements of the national historic preservation program and strongly influences the shape of state and even local preservation laws. The NHPA creates a comprehensive system for the identification, evaluation, protection, and enhancement of historic resources. It also provides an administrative structure to carry out these authorities.

At the center of the program is the National Register of Historic Places (hereafter "the Register"), which embraces the buildings, sites, districts, structures, and objects that are significant in U.S. history, archaeology, architecture, culture, and engineering at the national, state, and local level. Listing on the Register, or meeting the criteria of eligibility for it, is a basic prerequisite for a property to benefit from the NHPA's protections and assistance. The Register is administered by the Secretary of the Interior, acting through the National Park Service (NPS).

The Register caps a nationwide inventory process for identifying significant historic properties. Conducted primarily at the state level through individual state historic preservation officers (SHPO) in accordance with federal standards and criteria, surveys are ongoing to develop a nationwide database for planning and resource allocation decisions affecting historic properties.

Properties meeting the criteria of the Register are afforded protection through Section 106 of the NHPA. This requires that a federal agency "take into account" the effects on such properties of activities which it carries out, funds or otherwise assists or approves. When a historic property is affected, the agency must obtain the comments of the cabinet-level Advisory Council on Historic Preservation (hereafter "the Council").

The Section 106 process, set forth in regulations at 36 CFR (*Code of Federal Regulations*) 800, is the basic protection in U.S. federal law for historic properties. It applies to all properties on or eligible for the Register, regardless of ownership, as long as there is some federal involvement in the action affecting them. In practice, this is a conflict-resolution process, bringing together the project sponsor, preservation experts (the Council and the SHPO) and interested members of the public. Agreement is sought on measures that will preserve significant features of the historic resource but also allow the project to go forward.

Agreement is reached in the vast majority of cases. If there is no agreement, the Council issues formal comments to the head of the federal agency proposing the project. The agency is obligated to consider the comments in reaching a decision, but is not required to follow them. It is important to recognize that this system provides no final authority to veto a federal action that might destroy a historic property, regardless of the importance of the resource.

A related program provides for the recovery of historic and archaeological data threatened with loss as a result of a project with federal involvement. Under the Archeological and Historic Preservation Act of 1974 (16 USC 460), an agency must notify the Secretary of the Interior when significant data will be lost. The agency or Secretary is authorized to undertake recovery of the data, in accordance with specified standards, and project funds are allowed to be used for this purpose. This program is administered by the NPS.

For archaeological resources located on U.S. federal or Indian lands, substantially greater protections exist (Hutt 1994, Hutt et al. 1992). The Archaeological Resources Protection Act of 1979 (16 USC 470aa-mm) prohibits the unauthorized excavation of archaeological sites and artifacts on those lands, establishes civil and criminal penalties for violations, and requires the establishment of public archaeological awareness programs on federal lands. A permit system regulates the conduct of legitimate scientific investigations.

A final provision of general application to U.S. federal agencies is Section 110 of the NHPA. This obligates federal agencies to manage historic resources under their control in accordance with professional preservation standards and policies. In 1988, the NPS issued "Guidelines for Federal Agency Responsibilities under Section 110 of the National Historic Preservation Act" (53 FR [*Federal Register*] 4727). These complement the "Secretary's Standards and Guidelines for Archeology and Historic Preservation" (48 FR 44716), which generally apply to governmental activities affecting historic properties. Section 110 requirements were strengthened in the National Historic Preservation Act Amendments of 1992 (Public Law 102-575), which require federal agencies to establish preservation programs for the identification, evaluation, Register nomination, and protection of historic properties. Many First Americans sites are on lands owned or controlled (by license, permit, or financial support) by the federal government.

As noted earlier, particular provisions of U.S. federal law and regulation deal with the interests of Native Americans in historic resources. The regulations implementing Section 106 make special provision for the involvement of Indian tribes and other Native Americans in the project review process. Likewise, the Council has adopted specific policies regarding the treatment of human remains and grave goods in Section 106 cases. More specifically, the U.S. Native American Graves Protection and Repatriation Act of 1990 (NAGPRA; 26 USC 3001) legislated the ownership or control of certain types of Native American cultural items (including human remains and associated funerary objects, and unassociated funerary objects, sacred objects, and objects of cultural patrimony) excavated or discovered on federal or tribal lands. Ownership of these cultural items is assigned to Native lineal descendants or tribes or Native organizations in a designated priority order, and owners have the right to claim those items and request their return. First Americans human remains and associated funerary objects may be subject to Native repatriation under this law.

The American Indian Religious Freedom Act (AIRFA; 16 USC 1996) declares it to be the policy of the United States to protect the free exercise of traditional religions by American Indians and to provide access to sacred sites and the use of sacred objects. A second provision requires federal agencies to evaluate their programs to accommodate this policy. While this has not provided specific legal protection to traditional sites and objects, it has influenced the implementation of other federal preservation laws, such as the NHPA, and is occasionally referred to in regulations and guidelines relating to archaeological and historic preservation. The Religious Freedom Restoration Act of 1993 (42 USC 2000bb) says that the government should not "substantially burden religious exercise without compelling justification." This law is expected to strengthen agency consideration of the AIRFA policy statement in agency planning and operations.

In summary, the U.S. federal program provides for the identification of archaeologically and historically significant resources and ensures their careful consideration in the planning of federal and federally supported projects. Likewise, federally owned archaeological resources are given stringent protection against vandalism and looting. However, the reach of federal law to privately held resources is limited and its strictures only apply to the actions of federal agencies that may harm such properties.

State Historic Preservation Laws

The role of the state government is essentially threefold: it is a partner with the federal government in carrying out the provisions of federal law; an implementer of state preservation laws; and an authorizer for the conduct of preservation regulation at the local government level. The first role is embodied in the state historic preservation program, through which the SHPO participates in the survey and inventorying activities related to the expansion of the Register and plays an active role in the conflict-resolution process of Section 106.

The second role varies greatly from state to state. A number of states have project review processes similar to Section 106 of the NHPA, covering activities involving state agencies. These are often tied to state inventories of historic properties, similar to the Register but usually embracing a larger number of properties than the state has nominated to the federal list. Only a few states, though, extend these protections to private actions with no governmental involvement.

Closely related are state environmental policy acts, requiring consideration of the impacts of state and local government-sponsored projects on the cultural and natural environments. These laws customarily mandate environmental impact statements and often provide a mechanism for rejecting projects that have unacceptable impacts. They are often used to protect historic and archaeological resources.

Most states have enacted special laws for the protection of archaeological sites. Most common are laws that parallel the protections for federally owned lands. They establish a permit system for excavation on state-owned lands and often place the administration of the system under a designated state archaeologist. A few states have extended protection to private lands, requiring the consent of the owner before anyone disturbs an archaeological site.

A related area of state activity to protect archaeological resources extends to those resources located underwater. With authority from the federal Abandoned Shipwreck Act of 1987 (43 USC 2101), states now have title to historic shipwrecks within their jurisdiction and can issue permits to regulate salvage. The 1987 law clarified state authority and is expected to generate a number of new or revised state laws.

Another somewhat arcane area of law is also used for archaeological protection—legislation enacted to protect cemeteries. While not always specifically directed at historic cemeteries and burials, prohibitions on the disturbance of graves offer a legal tool that can be quite effective. Cemetery and unmarked burial laws are also found at the state (Price 1991) and local level.

Finally, under the U.S. Constitution those powers not given to the federal government are reserved to the states. As a result, the exercise of such authorities as the police power by local governments, which are creatures of the state, must be based on delegations of authority from the state government. Accordingly, the basis for local government regulation must be found in state constitutions or legislative enactments. Thus the state plays an important role in shaping the protection of historic resources at the local level.

Local Regulation of Historic Properties

It is at the local level of U.S. government that direct regulation of private activity affecting historic resources occurs. Consistent with state enabling legislation, general zoning authority, or constitutional provision, a local government may enact a system that requires approval from a governmental body before a private action is allowed to modify or destroy a historic property. This has been done in hundreds of communities throughout the United States.

Essentially, the protective process requires formal designation of a property as a local landmark and then establishes a governmental commission to review and approve proposed alterations or demolition. While this process can be used for individually listed properties, it is most often applied to historic districts. The extent of control may vary from simply delaying the proposed action for a period of time to allow negotiation to outright prohibition.

While these techniques have been primarily used to protect historic structures and neighborhoods, they have also been employed in some jurisdictions to protect archaeological resources. When so used, a similar public agency review occurs of proposed private action which may disturb a recognized archaeological site, leading to approval or disapproval.

A Private Law Approach to Preservation

The foregoing discussion has focused on public regulation to protect historic properties. One of the most effective tools for long-term preservation of historic and archaeological resources comes from consensual arrangements among private parties and government agencies (see Henry 1993). Through the use of easements or preservation restrictions, private properties are voluntarily removed from the threat of development.

An easement essentially is the surrender of certain development rights by the owner of a property, usually in exchange for money or some tax benefit. A holding organization, either a governmental body or nonprofit organization, is given the legal right to review proposed changes to a historic property or alterations are prohibited altogether.

These restrictions "run with the land," binding successive purchasers in accordance with the terms of the easement. As they are not imposed on an unwilling owner by a governmental body, they tend to be more successful in achieving their preservation objective. Easements are widely used to protect open space and archaeologically significant properties.

Summary: The U.S. Protective System

Protecting historic resources in the United States relies upon the interplay of three levels of government. While the standards for deciding what is significant are largely derived from the federal government, their application and the most effective imposition of controls occurs at the state and local levels. Only at the local level does the authority exist to absolutely prohibit the destruction of a privately owned historic property. However, the integration of historic preservation concerns into the planning of public projects is highly developed and achieves substantial success in accommodating development and preservation goals.

The Canadian Experience: A Brief Comparison

While Canada has a federal structure in many ways similar to that of the U.S., there are substantial differences in the governmental approach to preservation (see Magne, this volume). This stems from the constitutional assignment of all matters pertaining primarily to "property and civil rights" to provincial jurisdiction. The protection of historic properties is such a matter. As a result the national government's involvement with historic resources is limited to properties which it owns, properties in the territories, property officially declared to be "for the general advantage of Canada," and property involved in an undertaking over which the federal government has jurisdiction.

The national government has taken steps to protect those historic properties over which it has some jurisdiction. For example, in Canada the Federal Heritage Building Policy of 1982 establishes a preservation agency to oversee activities affecting "heritage properties" over forty years old. Its functions are akin to those of the United States' NPS with regard to the development of a register of historic properties, promotion of conservation at provincial and territorial levels, and management of historic properties. Like the U.S. Advisory Council, the Canadian Federal Heritage Building Review Office is charged with establishing criteria and procedures to evaluate plans for alterations and demolition of heritage properties.

Again as in the U.S., Canada has special protections for resources located on Indian reserves. Under the Indian Act, government approval is required for the acquisition of certain historic and archaeological resources associated with Indian culture, graves, and art.

While the role of the national government in protecting historic properties is substantially less than in the United States, substantial steps have been taken at the provincial level. Often these parallel the activities of states in the U.S., with some additional actions taken to compensate for the absence of national government authority. Provincial programs are similar to those in the U.S. states: effective preservation programs are based on an inventory of significant properties, evaluated against professional criteria, and then afforded protections in planning and through a regulatory process. The protective processes vary, but some provinces require that a specified amount of time elapse before a heritage resource can be altered and others extend more stringent forms of prior approval.

Archaeological resources are often given special protection, again in a manner similar to that in the United States. Protected sites may require government permits, and sometimes the consent of the owner, for excavation. Removal of artifacts from a province may be prohibited without provincial government approval.

Finally, many provinces recognize the importance of municipal control over historic properties. Provincial legislation may enable local governments to establish conservation advisory committees, which, like their U.S. counterparts, oversee the protection of heritage conservation districts.

In sum, the Canadian legal environment favors the application of preservation protections at the provincial and local level. The parallels with the U.S. experience are many, but the constitutional limitations on national government action result in important differences.

Conclusion: The North American Legal Landscape

The traditions of English common law have joined with a distinctly North American approach to the protection of private property rights and the decentralization of government to place a distinctive stamp on historic preservation law. While the national government may set general standards and criteria and take the leadership in a nationwide preservation program, effective regulation and protection of historic properties occurs at a level of government closer to the regulated property owner.

This does not necessarily result in a lower level of protection for historic properties, but does change the political dynamics of establishing and administering protective programs. Recognition of where the effective legislative and administrative decision making occurs is essential to the effective creation and use of legal tools to protect historic resources.

References Cited

Henry, Susan L.
1993 *Protecting Archeological Sites on Private Land*. U.S. Department of the Interior, National Park Service, Interagency Resources Division, Preservation Planning Branch, Washington.

Hutt, Sherry
1994 The Civil Prosecution Process of the Archaeological Resources Protection Act. U.S. Department of the Interior, National Park Service, *Archeological Assistance Technical Brief* No. 16.

Hutt, Sherry, Elwood W. Jones, and Martin E. McAllister
1992 *Archeological Resource Protection*. The Preservation Press, Washington.

Price, H. Marcus, III
1991 *Disputing the Dead. U.S. Law on Aboriginal Remains and Grave Goods*. University of Missouri Press, Columbia.

Archaeology's World: The Legal Environment in Asia and Latin America

Charles R. McGimsey III

Legal systems are, ultimately, statements of political philosophy, and no one political philosophy is held world wide. Nearly all countries in Asia and Latin America express, through legislation, a concern for cultural resources. In most instances a country asserts legal standing with respect to cultural resources because it recognizes that its archaeological and historical heritage is a key element in the delineation of its modern national identity. Most countries in Asia, but fewer in Latin America, assert outright ownership and nearly all endeavor to exert some measure of control through registration of sites, permits, or control of exportation of artifacts to foreign lands. Laws with international ramifications such as that of the United States on Importation of pre-Colombian Monumental and Architectural Sculpture or Murals and UNESCO conventions which, when adopted by a country, have the force of law are playing an increasing role as are paralegal documents such as UNESCO Recommendations and ICOMOS Charters.

In discussing the legal environment of archaeology it must be recognized at the outset that laws and legal systems are first, foremost, and forever political statements. Politics, in turn, is the art of the possible. Legal structures do have (fortunately) a certain inertia against the ebb and flow of popular opinion but they are, and in the end must be, a reflection and an expression of the strongest current cultural force. Sometimes that strength is expressed by raw power. More often it is an expression or a continuation of cultural tradition as adjusted by widespread, deeply felt, current goals. It may be that, "We hold these truths to be self evident," but if succeeding generations do not, the principles set forth in the U.S. Declaration of Independence and reflected in U.S. laws will be changed or abandoned.

The second important implication of the fact that laws are a statement of a publicly accepted philosophy is that no one philosophy is accepted world wide and therefore legal principles will tend to differ as philosophies and cultural histories differ. (However, attempts are continuing to develop, and have adopted, broadly accepted principles [see below]). There appear to be, world wide, three major legal philosophies or approaches:

Common Law systems are those based, like English law, on judicial decisions supplemented by often very detailed statutes on various topics. Most English-speaking nations, and those countries with legal histories closely associated with English-speaking nations, have such systems.

Civil Law or *Code Law* systems, based on Roman law, are generally codified in statutes which set forth general principles. These are then applied by judges to all areas of law.

Legal systems based on *Marxist/Leninist* social theory are somewhat similar in technique to Civil Law but their concept of property is distinct from Common Law.

All three of these legal philosophies are operative in the geographic areas under consideration here.

While nearly all countries in Asia and in Latin America express, through legislation, a concern about their cultural resources, the specifics vary widely and defy concise summarization. In most instances a country asserts legal standing with respect to its cultural resources because it recognizes that its archaeological and historical heritage is a key element in the delineation of its modern national identity. Only a very few countries (e.g., Paraguay) have made almost no realistic attempt to assert legal standing with respect to their archaeological resources. Others (e.g., China, Japan, Mexico, and Peru) devote considerable legislative attention to such resources. There is enormous variation in between.

National Legal Approaches

Most countries in Asia declare to one degree or in one manner or another outright state ownership of cultural resources (e.g., China assumes national ownership of all cultural objects underground or underwater) and/or they exert a high level of control over archaeological research (e.g., in Mongolia all research is subject to approval by the Academy). China and

Japan, in particular, emphasize planning (e.g., Japan requires advance notice, planning, and consultation whenever construction work will involve the excavation of any site well known to contain buried cultural property).

Almost all Asian countries try to restrict the outflow of cultural properties and many attempt to control excavation by various techniques such as permits, by the registration of sites, or by requiring the reporting of finds.

A number of Asian countries are particularly noted for their long-standing affirmative approach, as contrasted with restrictive legislation, in identifying and protecting their cultural resources. India and Pakistan have had an Archaeological Survey since it was established by the British in 1861. China, Japan, and Indonesia also have active national programs of research and protection.

Latin America, despite a long history of wholesale looting of its cultural resources, by foreigners and compatriots, from *conquistadors* to *huaqueros*, has not had a uniform attitude regarding the protection of the archaeological heritage. In some countries there is an emphasis on the archaeological heritage as a part of the national identity. In others, private interests have been able to restrict legislation affecting private property or preventing the destruction of archaeological resources by construction projects. Only a few countries appear to have really active positive programs. The programs in Mexico and Peru are perhaps most notable, but there are some others such as in Guatemala and Ecuador.

Overall, Mexico and Peru have devoted the greatest attention to their cultural resources. Mexico, like most Central American countries, assumes national ownership of all cultural monuments, but Panama has no such legislation, and Costa Rica concentrates on artifacts.

Peru assumes national ownership of all sites, but private landowners may retain property rights if the site is registered. Clandestine excavations are outlawed. Honduras "takes property [assumes national ownership] in all registered historic monuments and their contents and provides special protection of other items 'irrespective of their ownership'" (O'Keefe and Prott 1984:58), and in Ecuador and Argentina sites are declared to be state property. Elsewhere, ownership, or even control, is extremely varied and less clearly enunciated. For example, Brazil provides for registered sites, Chile requires permits for excavation at all National Monuments, and a number of countries assume national ownership of all artifacts discovered after specific established dates.

Controls over excavation by foreigners and/or over the export of artifacts are extremely widespread in Latin America with, again, Mexico and Peru having the most detailed regulations. In Peru it is stipulated that work may only be done by scientific organizations, that all artifacts are state property and must remain in the country, and that all research programs must incorporate local scientists and students.

The 1972 U.S. law on the Importation of pre-Columbian Monumental or Architectural Sculpture or Murals makes it illegal to import into the United States cultural items whose export is forbidden by Mexico, and Central and South American states. With respect to Asia, the UNESCO (United Nations Educational, Scientific, and Cultural Organization) convention on illicit import, noted below, can have a somewhat similar effect.

International Approaches

Legal approaches are unique to each country to a marked degree, but, particularly since World War II, there have been increasing efforts, through UNESCO and, more recently, through the International Council on Monuments and Sites (ICOMOS), to design and have adopted more universally accepted documents and guidelines.

Three UNESCO conventions have particular relevance to the protection of the archaeological heritage:

• Convention for the Protection of Cultural Property in the Event of Armed Conflict, 1954

• Convention on the Means of Prohibiting and Preventing the Illicit Import, Export and Transfer of Ownership of Cultural Property, 1970

• Convention for the Protection of the World Cultural and Natural Heritage, 1972

Conventions, by traditional international law, are "immediately binding on the states party to them, though they often cannot be invoked by individuals or groups within those states until they have been incorporated in national law" (O'Keefe and Prott 1984:75).

There are also fourteen UNESCO recommendations on cultural heritage, several of which have subsequently become conventions. Recommendations are not law but the International Court of Justice recognizes that "the teachings of the most highly qualified publicists of the various nations [are] subsidiary means for the determination of rules of law" (Statute of the International Court of Justice, Art. 38(c) and (d)). UNESCO recommendations would certainly seem to qualify under this criteria and thus become part of the general principles of law recognized by nations.

Finally, there is another set of documents which, like the UNESCO recommendations, constitute powerful consensus statements with direct relevance to the protection of the world's archaeological and historical heritage. These are the ICOMOS charters. Of general interest is the Charter for the Conservation of Historic Towns and Urban Areas, the so-called "Venice Charter," which has only recently been adopted. Of much greater potential relevance to archaeology is the Charter for the Protection of the Archaeological Heritage under development by the ICOMOS International Committee on Archaeological Heritage Management and adopted by the Ninth ICOMOS General Assembly, Lausanne, 1990. This document endeavors to set forth internationally acceptable guidelines with respect to legislation, inventories, research, curation, professional qualifications, and international cooperation which will be essential to us all as we work within a legal environment to carry out the most effective archaeological research, management, and conservation.

Acknowledgment

I am deeply indebted to P.J. O'Keefe and L.V. Prott (1984) for the majority of the specific legal details and many of the thoughts reported in this paper, but they cannot be held responsible for my interpretations.

Reference

O'Keefe, P.J., and L.V. Prott
1984 *Law and the Cultural Heritage, Volume 1, Discovery and Excavation.* Professional Books Ltd., Abingdon, Oxon.

Government Support of Archaeology in Canada

Martin P. R. Magne

When this paper was presented, Canada did not have federal archaeological resource management legislation. However, the Canadian Department of Communications is in process of completing a national review of archaeological legislation and policy, hopefully leading to draft legislation. Professional activity in Canada leading to the policy review is discussed, as are the key points which the federal policy makers are considering. The provincial experience, in particular that of Alberta, is presented as contrast and example. International recognition of Canadian sites and interpretive developments have created an environment of public appreciation for the value of proper archaeological resource management on which the Canadian government would be wise to capitalize.

The topic of government support for archaeology in Canada is timely, because the Canadian government is completing a full and long-awaited review of its archaeological heritage policy. As of the time this article went to press, Canada has no overriding archaeological protection and management legislation, but the Canadian Department of Communications staff have prepared legislative "drafting instructions" for their minister to bring to cabinet.

This article addresses this situation at some length, because there is a common perception that Canada has had a well developed public trust, a trust made public by thorough legislation, competent resource management, and intelligent and tasteful cultural tourism. In short, there is a perception that Canada is quite active in repaying its public trust. At the risk of seeming somewhat biased, I will contrast the federal situation with the Alberta experience, since I believe it instructive to illustrate what can be done with archaeology when a solid public trust does exist.

Federal State of Affairs in Canada

At present, Canada's archaeological sites on federal lands are not:

• Protected as archaeological sites, unless they are of five particular types on Indian Reserves[1] (Department of Indian and Northern Affairs Development Act 1967). There is no explicit protection offered for archaeological sites. Penalties for contravention of the Indian Act amount to a maximum fine of $200 or not more than three months in jail. In theory, one could remove a totem pole from a reserve, sell it to any number of dealers for a small fortune, and be fined $200.

• Necessarily subject to impact assessment or mitigation in event of development impacts.

• Under Crown trusteeship as a particular resource.

• Registered or managed by a central system. Canada at the moment has no central registry of archaeological sites on federal lands, no central list of archaeological research permits, and no central repository of archaeological reports (see CAA 1986:1)

It would, however, be misleading to say that Canada has no means whatsoever of managing its archaeological resources. Management of archaeological research and resources in Canada occurs at federal, provincial and municipal levels. Suffice it here to point out that the provinces, while not all equal, have led the way in archaeological protection, and have generally stringent and effective archaeological legislation and resource management agencies. Federal archaeology falls principally under two agencies: the Canadian Museum of Civilization (CMC) and the Canadian Parks Service (CPS). With no archaeological legislation, these agencies operate under museum and parks laws. The CPS, however, does have several policies concerning archaeological resources, including management guidelines and ministerial directives applying to

---

1. These include (a) Indian gravehouses, (b) carved grave poles, (c) totem poles, (d) carved house posts, and (e) rocks "embellished with paintings or carvings."

collections and human remains. Archaeological resources in the CPS are treated as significant resources in the environmental assessment and review process.[2]

Canada is now completing a large museum complex, the Canadian Museum of Civilization, which will likely cost over $300 million by the time it is complete. The CMC houses the Archaeological Survey of Canada (ASC) which, despite its name, is not mandated to manage all of the archaeological resources on federal lands. Rather, its task is one of research, collection, and exhibition; it is primarily museum- and education-oriented, although it also plays a role in management through its Rescue Archaeology Program. The northern territories, the Yukon and the Northwest Territories, while without archaeological legislation, operate regulatory and research bureaus under regulations pursuant to the acts which brought the territories into existence. These territories would like to obtain provincial status, and in turn develop their own antiquities or heritage legislations (see for example, Yukon Heritage Branch 1989) but will not be able to do so until they have true legislative bodies.

Role of the Canadian Archaeological Association

The Canadian Archaeological Association (CAA), the main professional archaeological organization in Canada, with a membership of about four hundred individuals, suggested in 1986 that the federal government institute a Canadian Antiquities Act with the following recommendations (CAA 1986: 7; see also Byrne 1988):

1. Incorporate the spirit and intent of the UNESCO (United Nations Educational, Scientific, and Cultural Organization) conventions of 1956, 1970, and 1972;

---

2. Since 1989, a new Canadian Environmental Assessment Act (CEAA) has been drafted and contains provisions for archaeological and traditional aboriginal resources. CEAA regulations, as well as inclusion and exclusion lists, are being prepared in anticipation of proclamation of the act in 1994.

2. Include all categories and aspects of *in situ* heritage resources;
3. Supersede all other federal legislation and regulations which relate to the development of federal lands and projects;
4. Clearly indicate that archaeological objects and the "archaeological subsoil" are the property of the Crown;
5. Provide for the management of national heritage resources;
6. Set out guidelines and procedures for heritage impact assessment and mitigation studies and provide basic standards for archaeological investigations; and
7. Establish a national advisory board with representation from heritage groups and the native peoples of Canada.

The CAA (1985) has also been active in calling for amendments to the Cultural Property Export and Import Act, the principal concern being that the act cannot actually *prevent* the export of archaeological items. The CAA also believes that since the process mandated by the act assigns monetary value to items for which export is being sought, it encourages illicit acquisition of archaeological artifacts. In 1985 the federal government replied that it did not see any need to amend that act, but instead recognized a need to institute policy "to inspire enactment of legislation." In truth, it is not known to what extent Canada's archaeological resources are endangered by U.S. or other foreign markets, but the U.S. experience to date is frightening. A general feeling among Canadian archaeologists is that increasing population pressures can only bring more of the horrors to our own backyard.

Current Policy Review

The CAA's lobbying efforts appear to have been successful. The federal archaeological policy review (Canada Department of Communications 1988) has engaged the efforts of four federal departments, a rare event indeed: Communications (principal policy development; CMC, ASC), Environment (CPS, archaeology units), Transport (cultural property export and import, harbors, railways) and Indian and Northern Affairs (Yukon and Northwest Territories, Indian Reserves, treaty considerations).

The total number of interventions submitted was, for a nationally distributed discussion paper, moderate: more than one hundred written briefs, most of which were very substantive, with general agreement at policy level. Native peoples have expressed great interest in the project, in particular Shuswap, Grand Treaty 3, and Dene. Again, there is general agreement, but Native groups have questions about comprehensive claims now in process, and about ownership (McGhee 1989c).

The communications department is acting swiftly. Marcel Masse, a member of Parliament, began an archaeological policy review when he was communications minister (see Masse 1986). In his absence, the process lagged considerably. Masse returned as minister in the late 1980s and began work on the legislation drafting process immediately. His 1986 remarks to the CAA led many to believe that he will champion this cause. One of Masse's senior officials at the 1989 Fredericton CAA meetings assured the CAA of Masse's personal commitment by expressing the desire to draft legislation which will (McGee 1989):

• Resolve the question of ownership of archaeological resources in areas of federal jurisdiction;

• Assure the inclusion of archaeological considerations in impact assessment procedures at the federal level (see footnote 2);

• Recognize the special importance of much of our archaeological heritage for Canada's aboriginal peoples and facilitate their active involvement in its protection, management, and interpretation;

• Enhance our capability to protect an archaeologically significant wreck by enabling the government to deal with it in a heritage context;

• Introduce further controls on the permanent export of archaeological objects from Canada;

• Develop mechanisms for archaeologists, as well as aboriginal peoples and other interest groups, to have input into federal archaeological resource management on an ongoing basis;

• Enhance public appreciation of and awareness about our archaeological heritage, through dissemination of information and public education; and

• Develop the organizational structure for the federal government to carry out its responsibilities respecting archaeological heritage.

The Alberta Example and the Role of the Public

While the federal government is only now preparing archaeological legislation, several Canadian provinces have had firm legislation in place for some time. Furthermore, the activity at the federal level appears to be addressing the professional viewpoint, but is it actually in tune with the wishes of the general public? The Alberta Historical Resources Act (AHRA; ADCM 1987) addresses those points which McGee (1989) had indicated were being considered for the federal act. The Alberta act specifies Crown ownership, requires "user pays" impact assessments, provides a public advisory board, explicitly recognizes a public education role, and allows for the establishment of appropriate agencies. The AHRA was made possible by a series of public hearings and a public opinion survey organized by the Environment Conservation Authority (ECA) of Alberta in 1972 (ECA 1972). Some 74 submissions by individuals and organizations were instrumental in detailing what was perceived to be lacking and what were perceived to be real needs for legislation in Alberta. The public opinion poll showed, for example, that only 4 percent of respondents were not concerned with the matter. Forty-seven percent thought that the government should own the resources rather than the finder and family or finder only until death. The need to institute formal education was highlighted by 85 percent of respondents indicating that such education should start in grades 1 and 2. These findings would no doubt be even more strongly reflected in the sentiments of today.

Alberta's legislation and management structure were formed with foresight. The AHRA protects paleontological and natural historic resources as well as archaeological and historic period resources. Alberta recognized that the field of archaeology was emerging in the province in the late 1980s when the AHRA became law; thus the Archaeological Survey of Alberta (ASA) was created with both research and resource management sections. Other provincial government agencies maintain a resource management role only, leaving government-based research to museums. It has become clear to us that part of developing a public trust is justifying the need for archaeology, and resource management agencies alone cannot do that. A thorough master plan has allowed for thematic planning, leading to the opening of Head-Smashed-In Buffalo Jump in 1987, with visitation reaching 250,000 in a year and a half. Other major themes are currently undergoing capital development, for example the fur trade is being treated at Fort Dunvegan and Fort George/Buckingham House. One aspect of Head-Smashed-In which is of particular note is the very integral role of Natives in exhibit design, ongoing interpretation, and field archaeology. The Strathcona Archaeological Centre in Edmonton, also with a strong Native component, was the first of its type in Canada: a center where the general public could visit and volunteer in an archaeological program, year after year. Research undertaken by the ASA has a public component as well. For example, the First Albertans Project, a series of investigations into the initial peopling of the province, is making great use of private artifact collections everywhere from the southeastern parts of the province to the northwest.

Effects of Legislation on Private Citizens

Legislation mandating Crown control of historical resources affects private citizens, groups, organizations, companies, and government departments. In most provinces, this applies to both private and Crown lands. Federal legislation should also require private interests to undertake archaeological impact assessments at their own expense in situations where resources are known to be or even suspected of being endangered. In Alberta, there is very little resistance to this condition, and there is evidence that the costs of archaeological impact assessment are a marginal expense. For example, a study in 1980 (Donahue

1987) showed that the average cost of intensive archaeological excavations in subdivision areas of Calgary was about $8 per house, or about .01 percent of the cost of an $80,000 house, at a time when building profits had reached 17 percent. Some companies regularly do more research than they are required to do by legislation, often out of interest as much as to ensure that there will be no impacts.

In short, we need to consider the effects of such legislation on the general public as well as on the resource itself, or on professional interests. What will a new law say about ownership of archaeological specimens? What should happen to chance discoveries? Will surface collection be explicitly forbidden, partially controlled, or ignored? Will avocationalists have a clear role? Will Native groups? The Canadian government is undoubtedly thinking carefully about how to institute mechanisms to deal with private and government developers, to efficiently process reviews, issue assessment requirements, oversee fieldwork, receive reports, and allow development, or require mitigation, and close files. It is hopefully also aware that these mechanisms will require their own artifact and records curation systems. It must also realize that the private business community, particularly archaeological consulants and the travel industry, would benefit from a firm legislative base.

Prospects for the Canadian Heritage Future

Provincial governments by and large are doing their job in supporting archaeology in Canada, and the federal government is making moves to show that it is trying to catch up. If one looks around at the major players in Canadian archaeology, though, the universities could surely be doing more to educate their students about resource management. How many Canadian anthropology or archaeology departments teach the essentials of cultural resource management, even to graduate students, those who will need such knowledge the most? How many students are even aware of the federal policy review now in process, or even have the faintest idea of why federal legislation is necessary? It is obvious that resource management archaeology is still perceived widely in the universities as a stigma best ignored, or seen solely as a source of summer income among faculty and students alike.

The federal government of Canada appears to be overcoming inertia and getting the legislative ball rolling and one can hope that Canada has learned much from the experiences of its own provinces and other countries. Appropriate legislation for Canada would combine elements of the U.S. Moss-Bennett bill[3], National Historic Preservation Act[4], Archaeological Resources Protection Act[5] and Abandoned

---

3. The Archeological and Historic Preservation Act of 1974 (Public Law [P.L.] 93-291, 16 U.S. Code [U.S.C.] 469) amended the Reservoir Salvage Act of 1960 and requires federal agencies to notify the Secretary of the Interior if they think an agency-authorized construction project will affect archaeological resources; to conserve those resources, either themselves or with the assistance of the secretary; and to use up to 1 per cent per project of authorized project funds to conduct such conservation efforts. Subsequently, Sec. 208 of the National Historic Reservation Act Amendments of 1980 (P.L. 96-515) authorized a mechanism for exceeding that 1 percent limit. Funds for secretarial assistance were authorized in the 1974 legislation but have never been appropriated by the U.S. Congress.

4. The National Historic Preservation Act of 1966 as amended (16 U.S. C. 470; see Fowler, this volume) authorized a National Register of Historic Places (Register) and Advisory Council on Historic Preservation (Council). It requires that U.S. federal agencies inventory their lands and nominate all eligible properties to the Register and exercise caution in managing all properties that might be eligible for the Register, and consult with the Council about proposed agency-authorized undertakings that might impact properties on the Register or eligible for inclusion. "Historic properties" are defined as significant archaeological, architectural, engineered, landscaped, or traditional cultural sites that are at least fifty years old or are of exceptional significance.

5. The Archaeological Resources Protection Act of 1979 as amended (16 U.S.C. 470aa-mm) requires permits for removal of archaeological resources greater than one hundred years old from U.S. federal or tribal lands, authorizes criminal and civil penalties for unpermitted removal of such material, and requires U.S. federal land-managing agencies to establish archaeological public awareness programs.

Shipwreck Act[6] with a similar but stronger absolute ability to compel Canadian federal and federally funded agencies to undertake resource management studies and conservation efforts. Canada's experience with Native interests and past cooperation with Natives in archaeology have been good, though it has been pointed out recently that Pan-Nativism may result in a call for Native ownership of all North American archaeological artifacts of aboriginal origin[7]. This perspective, one that is not universal to Native peoples, fails to recognize that most archaeologists do not want to own the artifacts, but simply to have access to them. Professional archaeologists value not the objects themselves, but the knowledge which is gained from their study, their context, their meaning. Archaeologists certainly do not wish to prevent the existence of other points of view, but do want the freedom to express their own perspectives.

I have been told that the North American Free Trade Act (NAFTA), which was recently enacted in the spirit of great cooperation between our two countries, did not occasion any amendments to the Cultural Property Export and Import Act. That is perceived, I believe generally among Canadian archaeologists, as an error with potential detriment to Canadian, as well as American, heritage. Echoing Robert McGhee's request to the Society for American Archaeology (McGhee 1989a), I support a firm position against archaeological free trade.

Canada has succeeded in having a fair share of UNESCO World Heritage Sites designated, three of which are archaeological: Head-Smashed-In Buffalo Jump in Alberta, Ninstints on the Queen Charlotte Islands, and L'Anse Aux Meadows in Newfoundland. Alberta's successful development of Head-

---

6. The Abandoned Shipwreck Act of 1987 (43 U.S.C. 2101-2106) defines the legal status of abandoned shipwrecks as historic properties owned by the U.S. federal or state legal entity on whose submerged lands the wreck is embedded.
7. In the United States, the Native American Graves Protection and Repatriation Act of 1990 (25 U.S.C. 3001-3013, 18 U.S.C. 1170) assigns ownership of U.S. Indian, Native Alaskan, and Native Hawaiian human remains, associated funerary objects, and items of cultural patrimony from public and Indian lands to related Natives.

Smashed-In and the Tyrrell Museum of Palaeontology and the Queen's dedication of Wanuskewin Park in Saskatoon, along with the opening of the Canadian Museum of Civilization, create a wide awareness of historic, heritage, and archaeological issues. The Canadian government must surely realize that it cannot afford *not* to enact powerful archaeological legislation, for this is the only way it can develop the economic potential that cultural tourism is known to have. The future of a Canadian national archaeological public trust is here now (Bruck et al. 1986), and the mood should be capitalized upon, since a public logic may not be created again so easily, nor perhaps so well.

Postscript, March 1994

Interventions by and consultations with Canadian Aboriginal peoples led to reexamination of the proposed federal archaeology legislation, particularly sections dealing with ownership (for example, see Dunn 1991). With the support of the Archaeological Resource Management Branch, then of the Canadian Department of Communications, now with the Department of Canadian Heritage, the Canadian Archaeological Association formed the Canadian Archaeological Association Aboriginal Heritage Committee with a three-year mandate (1992/93–1994/95) to undertake nationwide consultation with First Nations peoples. The status of the proposed federal Canadian archaeological legislation as of 1992 is summarized in Byrne (1992).

Acknowledgments

My thanks to Bill Byrne and Jack Ives for comments, although the ideas expressed herein are entirely my responsibility. Ruthann Knudson gratefully provided details concerning U.S. legislation.

References Cited

Alberta Department of Culture and Multiculturalism. (ADCM)
1987 *Historical Resources Act*. Queen's Printer, Edmonton.

Bruck, P. A., I. Taylor, V. Blundell, R. Phillips, and others.
1986 *Archaeology and the Canadian Publics*. The Centre for
   Communication, Culture and Society. Carleton University,
   Ottawa.

Byrne, W. J.
1988 Letter to Charles McGee, Director General, Heritage Policy
   and Programmes, Department of Communications, Ottawa.
   CAA Newsletter 8(2):16-19.

1992 Status of Federal Archaeology Legislation. *CAA Newsletter*
   12(1)7-8.

Canadian Archaeological Association (CAA)
1985 The Cultural Property Export and Import Act and Canadian
   Archaeology: A Discussion Paper. Ms. distributed to CAA
   membership. CAA Archives, Archaeological Survey, Provincial
   Museum of Alberta, Edmonton.

1986 The Need for Canadian Legislation to Protect and Manage
   Heritage Resources on Federal Lands. *CAA Newsletter* 6 (1): 1 - 8.

Department of Communications
1988 *Federal Archaeological Heritage. Protection and Managment, A
   Discussion Paper*. Government of Canada, Ottawa.

Department of Indian and Northern Affairs
1967 *Department of Indian and Northern Affairs Development Act*.
   Government of Canada, Ottawa.

Donahue, P.
1987 Comments. In *Rescue Archaeology*, edited by R. L. Wilson, pp.
   165-166. Southern Methodist University Press, Dallas.

Dunn, M.
1991 *A National Overview of the Department of Communications
   Consultation with Aboriginal Peoples on Canadian Archaeological
   Heritage*. Canadian Department of Communications, Ottawa.

Environment Conservation Authority (ECA)
1972 *The Conservation of Historical and Archaeological Resources in
   Alberta*. Environment Conservation Authority, Edmonton,
   Alberta.

Masse, M.
1986 The Speech by the Honourable Marcel Masse, M. P. for
     Frontenac, Minister of Communications, at the Annual
     Conference of the Canadian Archaeological Association,
     Toronto, April 26, 1986. *CAA Newsletter* 6 (2): 19-22.

McGee, C.
1989 Notes for a Speech by Charles McGee, Director General,
     Museums and Heritage, Department of Communications, to the
     22nd Annual Conference of the Canadian Archaeological
     Association (CAA), May 13, 1989, Fredericton, New Brunswick.
     Ms., Information Services, Canadian Department of
     Communications, Ottawa, distributed to CAA membership.

McGhee, R.
1989a Letter to Dena Dincauze, President, Society for American
     Archaeology. Canadian Archaeological Association Archives,
     Archaeological Survey, Provincial Museum of Alberta,
     Edmonton.

1989b Who Owns Beringia? Paper presented to the 22nd Annual
     Meeting of the Canadian Archaeological Association,
     Fredericton, New Brunswick. *Canadian Journal of Archaeology*.
     13:13-20.

Yukon Heritage Branch
1989 *Managing the Yukon's Archaeological Resources: Towards an
     Archaeology Policy for the North*. A response to "Federal
     Archaeological Heritage Protection and Management: A
     Discussion Paper." Heritage Branch, Department of Tourism,
     Government of the Yukon, Whitehorse.

An Environment Out of Balance

Dennis C. Le Master

Public policy for archaeological resources is considered using a mosaic analogy. Subsequently, five processes in which public policy is formulated in the federal government are identified and described. Use by the Reagan administration of the appropriations process in formulating public policy is featured. A pessimistic view of the possible application of the Public Trust Doctrine in resolving conflicts over archaeological resources is offered in closing.

Natural resource management at the federal level in the United States is mainly determined by the policies under which it operates, and they are the sum of the principles, both implied and expressed, contained in a host of natural resource laws, administrative rules, court decisions, presidential budget requests, and congressional appropriations acts.

Natural resource policy is continually evolving, usually incrementally, through a complex interaction of economic, political, and other social forces, in the context of existing scientific knowledge and technology. Conflict is a frequent feature of change in natural resource policy, and as a result, changes in policy tend to be accepted in stages by the people and groups they affect.

After reviewing laws, administrative rules, court decisions, presidential budget requests, and congressional appropriations acts dealing with archaeological resources, I am confident the foregoing descriptive statements on natural resource policy also apply to archaeological resource policy, and in the same way that natural resource policy affects natural resource management, archaeological resource policy affects archaeological resource management.

So consider public policy for archaeological resources as a mosaic of policy statements contained in laws, administrative rules, court decisions, recent presidential budget requests, and congressional appropriations acts, with the different hues indicating the relative importance of the statements. Once that is done, consider the mosaic evolving sometimes slowly, sometimes rapidly, like a child's kaleidoscope. Having completed this exercise, one may have a better appreciation of the context and complexity, the metes and bounds, of public policy as it concerns archaeological resources.

Public Policy Processes

In a representative democracy characterized by separation of powers and federalism, public policy is formulated in several established, formal processes. There are five such processes in the United States, at least one in each of the three branches of government. Most familiar is the authorizing process—the process by which laws are made and federal programs established—located in the legislative branch, Congress. There is no equivocation here. Article I of the Constitution is clear: All legislative powers are vested in the Congress. Public policy is also formulated in the legal process through court decisions. Of course, the organizational *situs* of this process is the judicial branch. Less familiar, however, are the three remaining processes in which public policy is formulated, namely: the rule-making process, the process by which the president's annual budget request is developed and prepared, and the congressional appropriations process. The first two are located in the executive branch and the latter in the legislative branch. Rules can be defined as executive branch agency statements designed to implement, interpret, or prescribe law or to describe the organization, procedure, or practice requirements of the agency.

All five processes have multiple decision points. Citizens can participate in at least three of them—the authorizing process, the rule-making process, and the appropriations process. And they often do, sometimes alone, more often in or through groups. They write letters and statements for the record and appear as witnesses during public hearings in the authorizing and appropriations processes. More actively engaged citizens may even participate in some of the bargaining and coalition building that often accompanies congressional consideration of legislation. In the rule-making process, interested citizens can submit written views on a rule within a stipulated time period, and they may have the opportunity to present an oral argument. Citizens also have access to the legal process. They can sue, but usually to do so they must have "standing," a sufficient stake in a justiciable controversy to obtain judicial resolution. For example, to sue the federal government for some action on its part, one has to show injury, economic or otherwise, for the court to be willing to consider the suit. The process used in developing and preparing the president's annual budget request to Congress is the only process of the five which is inaccessible to the public. Actually, "inaccessible" is probably too strong a characterization. After all, presidential candidates and their policies are subject to public scrutiny and voting every four years.

The environment in which public policy is formulated in the United States is incredibly open and accessible, and I would encourage you to participate. There are so few who feel strongly about archaeological resources. There is a large and growing threat of huge environmental disasters occurring on our planet, due in large part to excessive human population growth, and I think archaeologists have some important scientific evidence to offer policy makers on what happens when a human population grows beyond that which its environment and technologies can sustain.

Having encouraged participation, I should also caution that appearances and reality are sometimes very different in public policy. For example, one of the most effective strategies of the Reagan administration was to formulate policy in the development and preparation of the president's budget request and the congressional appropriations process and to avoid the authorizing process. When he was director of the Office of Management and Budget, David Stockman frequently spoke of "zeroing out a program," understanding very well that a program without funding is effectively no program at all and that this technique was an easy way by which an administration can rid itself of a program at odds with administration policy.

Policy Formulation in the Budgeting Process

During the U.S. presidential campaign of 1980, Ronald Reagan promised to cut both taxes and non-defense spending, increase defense spending, and balance the budget. Taxes were cut substantially by the Kemp-Roth Tax Bill (more accurately, the Economic Recovery Tax Act of 1981). So was non-defense spending. But given the size of the tax cut and the increase in defense spending, as well as the magnitude of outlays associated with entitlement programs, the federal budget could not be brought into balance, even with repeated major cuts in various areas of non-defense spending. The result was unprecedented deficits, a huge (2.5 times) increase in the federal debt, and a relative doubling of interest payments by the federal government to service its debt.

These changes are summarized in Table 1, which contains data on the percentage distribution of budget outlays with respect to the four largest budget superfunctions of the federal government for fiscal years 1977 through 1988. Two major trends are evident beginning in fiscal year 1980. First, both national defense and net interest payments increase as a percentage of total outlays. Second, both human resources and physical resources decrease until fiscal year 1987, in the case of the former, and fiscal year 1988 in the case of the latter.

The effects of these policies were adverse to federal natural resource and environmental programs. "Natural resources and environment" is one of the 21 functional categories of the federal budget, as well as one of five components of the "physical resources" superfunction. Data on the natural resources and environment function are contained in Table 2 for fiscal years 1977 through 1988. The trend is obvious. Outlays for natural resources and the environment declined as a percentage of the total. They even declined in nominal dollars for fiscal years 1981 and 1984. The effects were adverse to archaeological resources, for most of the programs to protect them are included in the natural resources and environment function.

The same conclusion can be reached by examining budget authority—congressional authority given a federal agency to enter into commitments that result in spending—and outlays

Table 1. Outlays by Superfunctions as a Percentage of Total Outlays, FY 1977-1988.

Year	National Defense	Human Resources	Physical Resources	Net Interest
1977	23.8	54.2	10.0	7.3
1978	22.8	52.8	11.5	7.7
1979	23.1	53.1	10.7	8.5
1980	22.7	53.0	11.2	8.9
1981	23.2	53.4	10.5	10.1
1982	24.9	52.1	8.3	11.4
1983	26.0	52.7	7.1	11.1
1984	26.7	50.7	6.8	13.0
1985	26.7	49.9	6.0	13.7
1986	27.6	48.6	5.9	13.7
1987	28.1	50.0	5.5	13.8
1988	27.3	50.1	6.4	14.3

Source: Office of Management and Budget. 1986 *Historical Tables: Budget of the United States Government. FY 1987*, Table 3.2. Government Printing Office, Washington.

1. The superfunctions "national defense" and "net interest" are the same as the functions of the same titles. The superfunction "human resources" is the sum of the following functions: education, training, employment, and social services; health; social security and medicare; income security; veterans benefits and services. The superfunction "physical resources" is the sum of the following functions: energy, natural resources and environment, commerce and housing credit, transportation, and community and regional development.

for the Department of the Interior for fiscal years 1977 through 1988, as contained in Table 3. Both budget authority and outlays declined as a percentage of total budget authority and outlays. The Department has had relatively less money than it did in the 1970s to carry out its responsibilities, and its considerable responsibilities with regard to archaeological resources are among them.

Little change is likely in the foreseeable future for a turnaround of funding for the natural resources and environment function until the size of the debt is reduced and there is more "slack" in the budget, "slack" in the sense that the relative size of interest payments has declined and high priority programs have received significant funding increases.

Table 2. Outlays of the Natural Resources and Environmental Function, FY 1977-1988.

Year	Millions of Dollars	Percent of Total Outlays
1977	10,032	2.5
1978	10,983	2.4
1979	12,135	2.4
1980	13,858	2.4
1981	13,568	2.0
1982	12,998	1.7
1983	12,672	1.6
1984	12,593	1.5
1985	13,357	1.4
1986	13,639	1.2
1987	13,363	1.3
1988	14,606	1.4

Source: Office of Management and Budget. 1986 *Tables: Budget of the United States Government, FY 1987*, Table 3.1. Government Printing Office, Washington.

Table 3. Budget Authority and Outlays for the Department of the Interior, FY 1977-1988.

Fiscal Year	Budget Authority[1]	Percent of Total Budget Authority	Total Outlays[1]	Percent of Outlays
1977	3,741	.8	3,216	.8
1978	4,643	.9	3,878	.8
1979	4,770	.8	4,174	.8
1980	4,678	.7	4,477	.8
1981	4,408	.6	4,461	.7
1982	3,810	.5	3,948	.5
1983	4,956	.6	4,552	.6
1984	4,917	.5	4,947	.6
1985	5,016	.5	4,825	.5
1986	4,589	.4	4,789	.5
1987	5,279	.5	5,050	.5
1988	5,246	.4	5,147	.5

Source: Office of Management and Budget. 1989 *Historical Tables: Budget of the United States Government. FY 1990*, Tables 4.1, 4.2, 5.2, 5.3. Government Printing Office, Washington.

1. Millions of dollars.

Public Trust Doctrine

Having offered this rather gloomy prediction, I might as well offer another one on the application of the Public Trust Doctrine as a solution to conflicts between public and private use of natural resources and in federal public land law.

Professor Joseph L. Sax (1970) proposed in a seminal law review article that the doctrine be applied to natural resources. His intent was to encourage greater use of the legal process in formulating public policy on natural resources, and he envisioned the Public Trust Doctrine as a means to do so. This doctrine is based on the idea that public access to or use of some resources is sufficiently fundamental and important that the courts must use governmental action to protect against their expropriation by a private individual or group. A public trust problem typically arises when the interests of a diffuse majority are made subservient to the interests of a concerted minority as a result of a decision by a legislative or administrative body of government. Three elements need to be present: (1) the interests of a diffuse majority; (2) the interests of a concerted minority; and (3) some form of governmental action. In other words, the Public Trust Doctrine is very much a matter of cause and effect with the agent of the cause being government and the effect being one in which a recognized public interest is made subservient to a private interest.

Some members of the conservation community believe the doctrine is capable of a much broader application, including, at the extreme, addressing traditional conflicts between public and private use of natural resources. Such a belief seems to be misguided. Application of the Public Trust Doctrine has been narrow historically. Granted that it has been more broadly used in recent years, it still remains a very measured and carefully delineated doctrine. The doctrine does not, as Professor Charles F. Wilkinson puts it, "allow judges to act as roving ambassadors on behalf of a 'public' consisting mainly of environmentalists" (Wilkinson 1980). Nor, if the doctrine were applied to archaeological resources, would it extend such permission to archaeologists. If the principal problem concerning archaeological resources is their protection on private lands, the Public Trust Doctrine would provide little succor. For, if, as Wilkinson wrote, "The federal public lands are at the outer reaches of the public trust doctrine," then private lands have to be beyond it.

Conclusion

Nevertheless, the issue of the applicability of the Public Trust Doctrine seems irrelevant to the larger one, which is the protection and conservation of archaeological resources. Certainly, there is an overriding public interest in these resources; certainly, government as an agent of the public has an important responsibility for these resources. Given the level of human development activities in the world, which will continue to grow as human population grows, the needs in archaeological resource management overwhelm the means available for implementing existing policies—if they do not overwhelm the very policies themselves. This is the legal environment, and it is clearly out of balance with the need. The challenge of correcting this is both immediate and awesome.

References Cited

Sax, J.L.
1970 The Public Trust Doctrine in Natural Resources Law: Effective Judicial Intervention. *Michigan Law Review* 68:471-566.

Wilkinson, C.F.
1980 The Public Trust Doctrine in Public Land Law. *U.C. Davis Law Review* 14:269-316.

V. Public Education

The following papers deal with educating various segments of the public about archaeology. The collective message contained in these articles is that there are constituencies or potential constituencies that need to be won over to see that our common human heritage is protected and used wisely by the archaeological community for our mutual benefit. McManamon and Knudson describe the sources of widely distributed archaeological information available from U.S. government sources, and Gallant describes public media involvement with archaeological information in the United States. Devine discusses public school curricula that deal with archaeology, and Bense discusses public-private partnerships developed in Florida to conserve prehistoric and historic archaeology.

First Americans resources are sometimes spectacular, such as the 9-inch-long Clovis bifaces from the Richey cache in Washington State, but they are often undistinguished paleoenvironmental resources such as pollen cores from peat bogs and lake beds, paleosols, or insects. Average citizens in North and South America and northeastern Asia have a major part in protecting all of these resources, through their support of laws, government programs, museums, and field and laboratory research, and their involvement in land use plans and programs. They need to understand what archaeology and paleoenvironmental resources are, and the conservation needs of those resources. These papers discuss ways of educating that public about First Americans and other archaeological resources. Education is a critical element in wise stewardship of a public trust.

Bennie C. Keel
Ruthann Knudson

Public Archaeological Information from U.S. Government Sources

Francis P. McManamon & Ruthann Knudson

Information about public archaeology in the United States is available from various government sources, and much of this is relevant to First Americans research. Actual field survey or excavation reports, laboratory analytical data, and even occasional syntheses, when supported by federal land-managing agencies, are often available at no cost. In addition, there are several national archaeological information exchange efforts in place or being developed, including special publications, clearing houses, technical information series, training programs, and online databases.

National Archaeology Program Information Exchange

In the United States, the Secretary of the Interior is responsible for providing leadership and coordination for all federal archaeological activities. Over 25 federal agencies participate in the *federal archeology program*, but few produce public information about how to manage archaeological resources and what specific archaeological information is available from which agencies. To fulfill these services, the Secretary of the Interior has delegated federal archaeological leadership and coordination responsibility to the National Park Service (NPS) through the Departmental Consulting Archaeologist (DCA). The NPS Archeological Assistance Division (AAD), in Washington, D.C., provides staff support for the DCA and archaeologists in five NPS regional offices also take part in these activities. Together these elements form the NPS Archeologi-

This paper is adapted from a paper entitled "Public Information for Archeology from Government Sources," presented by George S. Smith, Francis P. McManamon, and Richard C. Waldbauer at the First World Summit Conference on the Peopling of the Americas, 1989.

cal Assistance Program (AAP). The AAP provides archaeological coordination and leadership on behalf of the Secretary and implements national archaeological goals and objectives with other international, federal, tribal, state, and local agencies and the private sector. Because the effective sharing of information is such an important aspect of efficient archaeological resource protection, interpretation, and management, the AAP has implemented a number of information exchange efforts including special publications, clearing houses, technical information series, training programs, and databases (McManamon et al. 1990).

A special 36-page issue of the NPS's *CRM Bulletin* (now simply titled *CRM*) on "Archeology and the Federal Government" was published in July 1988 and updated in 1994 (De Carlo et al. 1994). It provides the most comprehensive summary available of archaeological programs in various federal agencies, along with a summary of the federal statutes that affect archaeological preservation and thumbnail sketches of several federal archaeological projects. This publication describes the basis for and diversity of U.S. federal archaeology and provides summaries of positive highlights.

The Listing of Education in Archeological Programs (*LEAP*) clearing house is a computerized database identifying archaeological public education efforts around the United States. Information is solicited by AAD from federal agencies, but also from tribal, state, local, and private organizations. *LEAP* contains information about projects or programs to protect archaeological resources and educate the public about those resources, including avocational field and laboratory work, museum displays and exhibits; and brochures, posters, radio and television coverage, and films/video/audios about archaeology. Reports on clearing house information received in 1987 through 1989 (Knoll 1990), and 1990 through 1992 (Knoll 1993) have been published.

To foster communication among archaeologists in federal regional, tribal, state, or local agency offices and with the academic and international communities, the *Federal Archeology Report (FAR)* was developed by the AAP in 1988. This is a quarterly publication, and in 1994 it was distributed at no charge to nearly eight thousand individuals, including international individuals and agencies. Information related to First Americans research is occasionally mentioned, but probably of greater importance to First Americans scholars is its information about public archaeological programs that affect First Americans resources.

In 1986, the AAD initiated the *Archaeological Assistance Studies* with a report on methods and results of cost analysis for archaeological investigations. A second study, this one on archaeological education programs, was published in 1991. Since 1988, the AAD has produced a series of *Archaeological Assistance Technical Brief*s on a variety of topics: site stabilization with filter fabric or revegetation, state archaeology weeks, archaeology in the National Historic Landmarks program, site protection by burial, a state archaeological registry program involving private landowners, the federal contracting process, archaeological volunteers, a national survey of state archaeological protection laws, the DCA peer review process, and the civil prosecution process under the Archaeological Resources Protection Act (ARPA).

The AAD also distributes without charge federal U.S. archaeological laws, regulations, and guidelines.

In 1984, the U.S. Congress provided funds to the NPS to improve the coordination of federal archaeological activities. One of the main efforts to accomplish this led to the development of the *National Archeological Database (NADB)-Network* (Canouts 1991, 1992), in large measure in response to an earlier Congressional report (U.S. General Accounting Office 1981) citing the critical need for increased efficiency in federal archaeological activities. *NADB* is a "database of databases," an interrelated set of publicly available data modules. In 1994 *NADB-Reports* and *NADB-NAGPRA* were online, and *NADB-Permits* and *NADB-Maps* were planned for addition in 1995-96.

NADB-Reports is expected by 1995 to include over 250,000 citations of reports of U.S. archaeological work, most of those investigations having been done on federal lands or as part of federally assisted land development. Almost all of these reports are part of the "grey literature" of minimally distributed reports that often include substantive data about First Americans as well as other archaeological resources. Occasionally the reference is for a report of which only a single copy was filed with the land-managing agency. *NADB-Reports* contains the following information: bibliographic reference (author, year, title of publication), location where the report is on file, summary of the report content (geographical location of the work reported, type of work performed, federal agency involved, and keywords about various aspects of the report). Archaeologists in AAP regional offices (Philadelphia, Denver, Atlanta, San Francisco, and Anchorage) serve as coordinators to establish partnerships for continued data entry and records maintenance. *NADB-Reports* became a nationally aggregated reports database accessible in 1992, with online support from the U.S. Army Corps of Engineers (USACOE). This is a critical source of information about First Americans resources. Providing access to the database through a read-only subscription by users is being evaluated, and international technology transfer opportunities are being investigated. Information about online access to the *NADB-Network* is available from AAD, National NADB Coordinator.

The AAD maintains a clearing house on cases of archaeological looting in the United States (*LOOT*: Listing of Outlaw Treachery), with summary information about prosecutions of individuals who have looted or vandalized archaeological sites. Prosecutions may be carried out under a variety of federal, tribal, state, and local statutes. Instances of ongoing investigations, trials, or appeals are not included in the *LOOT* record until cases are legally resolved and information is publicly available. Approximately 75 cases are listed in *LOOT* at present, and unfortunately new cases are continually being added to the database. At present *LOOT* records can be accessed only with the assistance of an AAD archaeologist.

Federal Archeology: The Current Program (Keel et al. 1989) is the first publication to provide useful quantitative summary information about federal archaeological activities. It uses information from 1985 and 1986 surveys of federal agencies to describe the kinds of archaeological activities undertaken as part of the national program, the reasons those activities have been undertaken, the results of those activities (at least in terms of sites identified and evaluated and areas investigated), and a variety of other topics. It began the effort to summarize information about the archaeological resource base on federal lands. Information on the 1987 federal archaeology program was published in 1993 (McManamon et al. 1993), and data and comparative analyses from 1988 through 1990 activities (Knudson et al. forthcoming) are in a draft report currently under review. The 1991-92 U.S. federal archaeological program is also under review and expected to be published in the near future. Each of these is available through the AAD. While these reports do not have much information specific to First Americans resources, they do provide overviews of the U.S. federal program in which much First Americans research is conducted (see Bonnichsen et al., this volume).

Federal Archaeology Field and Laboratory Reports

In the United States, millions of dollars of archaeological excavation, analysis, and reporting is done on federal lands, or on lands affected by federally funded, authorized, or licensed development projects. Reports of this work generally are produced in relatively limited quantities, but often are available from the sponsoring agency, e.g., USACOE, Bureau of Land Management, Bureau of Reclamation, NPS, Forest Service, Fish and Wildlife Service, Tennessee Valley Authority, Department of Transportation. With such a limited distribution, these reports are part of the "grey literature" for which NADB-Reports (described above) was developed.

Other Sources of Public Information

The NPS *Cultural Resources Management Bibliography (CRBIB)* consists primarily of research reports including technology and techniques that address cultural resources within units of the National Park System in the fields of history, historic architecture, ethnology, archaeology, and curation. In addition, it includes NPS planning documents (General Management Plans, Development Concept Plans, Interpretative Prospectuses, etc.) as well as journal articles, theses, and dissertations when they deal specifically with the cultural resources of a particular park. The *CRBIB* does not contain newspaper clippings, popular articles, or unpublished archival sources (diaries, field notes, correspondence, etc). Certain information may be restricted in order to protect cultural resources. Plans are to link this with *NADB-Reports*. *CRBIB* probably is of use to First Americans scholars, particularly those interested in areas encompassed by National Park units.

The NPS is developing a computerized *Cultural Sites Inventory (CSI)*, an inventory of prehistoric and historic archaeological resources in NPS units. The inventory will contain standardized resources information for use in park, regional, and Washington office NPS planning and management. The *CSI* is first and foremost a management database for improving the NPS's preservation, protection, and interpretation of park archaeological resources. Because information contained in the database is generally restricted from public disclosure under the provisions of the National Historic Preservation Act and ARPA, it would be available only through NPS archaeologists. It could contain information about First Americans resources.

The USACOE Waterways Experiment Station (WES) has developed an *Archaeological Sites Protection and Preservation Notebook (ASPPN)* under the auspices of the Corps Environmental Impact Research Program (EIRP). *Technical Notes* on various impacts, site burial, structural stabilization, soil and rock stabilization, vegetative stabilization, camouflage and diversionary tactics, site surveillance, stabilization of existing structures, faunal and floral control, signs, and inundation have been intermittently published since 1988 for inclusion in the *ASPPN*. Since 1987 the EIRP has also published a series of *Technical Reports* on archaeological site preservation techniques, including site burial, preservation of rock art, site preservation planning, and control of vandalism. For a list of available publications or technical assistance, contact the WES Center for Cultural Site Preservation Technology, Vicksburg, Mississippi.

The National Technical Information Service (NTIS) within the U.S. Department of Commerce is a repository for some of the "grey literature" listed in *NADB-Reports*, and for a fee it reproduces reports in its files. For instance, almost all of the archaeological projects funded by the USACOE are filed with the NTIS, as well as with the Defense Technical Information Service (DTIS). Many federal agency archaeology reports completed since 1975 are available through NTIS. The DTIS is maintained by the Department of Defense (DoD) and, like NTIS, includes cultural resource and archeological management reports, specifically including records of the DoD and its member services (U.S. Army [including the USACOE], U.S. Air Force, National Guard Bureau, U.S. Navy, and U.S. Marine Corps).

The Smithsonian Institution, National Museum of Natural History (NMNH) in Washington, DC, maintains the National Anthropological Archives (NAA). These archives contain anthropological and archaeological reports and other papers and graphic materials related to Smithsonian endeavors, or things donated by or related to U.S. anthropological scientists. Information about Smithsonian involvement in First Americans research by no-longer-active NMNH staff members is located there.

Training

Training in archaeological preservation and management theory, methods, and techniques is available for public or academic archaeologists or for non-archaeologists who manage programs or resources and thus can affect archaeological properties (including those of the First Americans). A directory of the training opportunities for cultural resource management through federal and state agencies, universities and colleges, and other organizations, is published annually by the NPS in *CRM*.

The AAD coordinates training courses in archaeological curation and collections management, archaeology for managers, conservation in field archaeology, and an overview of archaeological protection programs. These are generally 40-hour courses with a tuition fee, and are held in various parts of the country. In 1991, NPS regional offices sponsored a free workshop on site stabilization, a for-fee 3-day workshop on geophysics techniques in archaeology, a for-fee 2-day workshop on issues in public interpretation of archaeological materials and sites, and a free 2-day class on issues in the protection and interpretation of archaeological and cultural materials. The Federal Law Enforcement Training Center regularly teaches a 40-hour for-fee course on archaeological resource protection. The Museum of Florida History in 1992 offered a free 20-hour course in archaeology for public school teachers, and South Carolina held a minimal-fee 9-day workshop on public school classroom archaeology. The Society for American Archaeology's Public Education Committee now routinely offers teachers training in archeology in association with its annual meeting.

The Historic Preservation program in the Department of Anthropology at the University of Nevada has a series of for-fee 5- or 10-day courses including archaeology for managers; an overview of current archaeology methods, and techniques; geomorphology in archaeological analysis; an introduction to archives; lithics; presenting the past to the public; and theory in contemporary archaeology. The National Preservation Institute often offers a for-fee 1-day course on charitable donation of easements for land conservation and historic preservation, including archaeology. Many of these have direct relevance to First Americans studies.

The Archeological and Historic Preservation Act of 1974 required that federal agencies report on archaeological salvage projects, and these are generally published in relatively limited numbers (the "grey literature" listed in *NADB*). However, several hundred copies of most reports are routinely printed and distributed to the public at no charge by agencies such as the Bureau of Land Management, Bureau of Reclamation, USACOE, NPS, and U.S. Forest Service.

Information Access—The Future

An important U.S. federal archaeology goal is preservation of the archaeological record for the future. A linked goal is preparation and dissemination of accurate interpretations of archaeological topics understandable to the general public. These should be among the highest priorities for all archaeologists, no matter where they are or what their principal job, subject matter, or research concerns. It is a critical factor for future conservation of First Americans resources.

References Cited

Canouts, V.
1991 Computerized Information Exchange on the Local and National Levels. *Sites & Monuments: National Archaeological Records*, edited by C.U. Larsen, pp. 231-247. The National Museum of Denmark, Copenhagen.

1992 NADB—The National Archeological Database. *Federal Archeology Report* 5(3):1,6-9.

De Carlo, V., R. Knudson, J. Osborn, and K. Schamel (editors)
1994 Archeology and the Federal Government. *CRM* 17 (6).

Keel, B.C., F.P. McManamon, and G.S. Smith (compilers)
1989 *Federal Archeology: The Current Program. Annual Report to Congress on the Federal Archeological Program FY 1985 and FY 1986.* U.S. Department of the Interior, National Park Service, Washington.

Knoll, P.C. (editor)
1990 *Listing of Education in Archeological Programs: The LEAP Clearing house. 1987-1989 Summary Report.* U.S. Department of the Interior, National Park Service, Washington.

1993 *Listing of Education in Archeological Programs: The LEAP Clearing house. 1990-1992 Summary Report.* U.S. Department of the Interior, National Park Service, Washington.

Knudson, R., F.P. McManamon, and J.E. Myers (compilers)
forthcoming*The Federal Archeology Program.* U.S. Department of the Interior, National Park Service, Archeological Assistance Division, Departmental Consulting Archeologist, Washington.

McManamon, F.P., P.C. Knoll, R. Knudson, G.S. Smith, and R.C. Waldbauer (compilers)
1993 *Federal Archeological Programs and Activities*. U.S. Department of the Interior, National Park Service, Archeological Assistance Division, Departmental Consulting Archeologist, Washington.

McManamon, F.P., G.S. Smith, and R.C. Waldbauer
1990 The Present and Future Archaeological Assistance Program. *American Society for Conservation Archaeology, Proceedings 1989*, edited by P.S. Miller, D.E. Gelburd, and G.E. Alderton, pp. 49-62. American Society for Conservation Archaeology, Portales, New Mexico.

U.S. General Accounting Office
1981 *Are Agencies Doing Enough or Too Much For Archeological Preservation? Guidance Needed*. CED-81-61. U.S. General Accounting Office, Washington.

School Curriculum and Archaeology

Heather Devine

Is the study of archaeology relevant in a high-technology world? Although many curriculum developers might respond negatively, other educators have recognized the usefulness of archaeology as a vehicle for cognitive development. The role archaeological research plays in the study of native culture and in environmental protection has also been acknowledged. However, the future of archaeology in the school program hinges upon the ability of archaeologists to address the concerns of both educators and native peoples vis-à-vis educational goals, instructional planning, and educational materials development.

The topic of archaeology in education is extremely broad in scope. This paper is focused on the following aspects of school curriculum and archaeology:

- The influence of curriculum policy;
- Current trends in curriculum development;
- The role of the archaeologist in archaeology education; and
- Instructional media and archaeology.

Curriculum Policy

Curriculum development, implementation, and revision is an ongoing process, which is governed by world-wide trends governing day-to-day life. In response to these trends curriculum policy makers set educational goals that reflect what society determines its children need to become productive citizens. Over the last thirty years the educational system has experienced major shifts in curriculum philosophy in response to pivotal political, social, and economic events (Kantrowitz and Wingert 1989: 51-53). The most recent shift in curriculum direction has occurred largely as a response to world-wide economic factors. The threat of global competition and a shrinking job market at home have had a profound influence on curriculum policy in North America. The long-term health of nations is directly tied to a well-educated work force able to adapt to the demands of an economy based on high technology. School programming, therefore, must produce students who are scientifically and technologically literate (Keen 1988).

How does this shift to a technical and economic orientation affect archaeology curricula? As one might expect, the effect is somewhat negative. Despite the highly technical nature of modern archaeology, it is not viewed as a "hard" science in the sense that physics and chemistry are "hard" sciences, but as a social science. It is considered part of the humanities, and hence has a low status in the eyes of curriculum builders with a technological orientation.

Current Trends in Curriculum Development

There continue to be ample opportunities, however, to promote archaeology in the curriculum. The following areas of school programming where archaeology content could conceivably stage a comeback include environmental education; curricula that promote cognitive development; and intercultural education, particularly Native education.

Environmental Education

The stewardship of the environment is one area attracting a great deal of attention today. On the one hand, the depressed economic climate of the 1980s placed extraordinary pressure on policy makers to loosen environmental restrictions on industry as a means of promoting economic activity. On the other hand, there is increased public pressure to eliminate the kinds of industrial practices which have resulted in environmental disasters such as the *Exxon Valdez* incident.

Curriculum development in environmental education will have direct implications for archaeology curricula. Already some North American provincial and state departments of education are implementing environmental education programs

(Calgary Board of Education 1989). Environmental education programs provide archaeology professionals with the opportunity to incorporate content on historical resources legislation and the principles of cultural resource management as it pertains to natural resource development.

CURRICULUM AND COGNITIVE DEVELOPMENT

The field of archaeology has always held an attraction for teachers and students because of the treasure-hunting mystique so often associated with it. But now educators have also come to recognize the potential of archaeology as a vehicle for teaching research methods, group problem solving, and hypothesis formation and testing (Abell 1985, Dyche 1985, Dyer 1983, Hartman 1985 Risinger 1973, Wittich and Schuller 1979: 78-82, 87, 101).

Archaeology is a fascinating topic for most pupils, and the methods employed in archaeological research require the kinds of higher-level thinking skills that instructors wish to encourage in students. Archaeology is also a hands-on discipline that incorporates a number of diverse areas and can involve group problem solving. These characteristics of archaeology make it ideal for *all* student groups, though the time and budget constraints of the regular school program often prevent teachers from introducing topics such as archaeology.

It is possible that promotion of archaeology as a means to develop thinking skills may provide yet another avenue for archaeology professionals who wish to make inroads into more standardized school programs. Those eager to raise the profile of archaeology at the K-12 level might consider offering assistance to local curriculum developers in the planning of projects incorporating archaeological methods.

INTERCULTURAL/NATIVE EDUCATION

As our world grows smaller through increased travel and more sophisticated communications, countries which have had relatively homogeneous populations are discovering that they are ill equipped to meet the needs of racially diverse immigrant populations with different languages and value systems. As a result school systems, governments, and, to a lesser extent, private industry, have responded by instituting policies and programs which recognize this new multicultural reality.

In Canada, this surge in multicultural awareness has brought with it a belated recognition of the unique cultural identity of the indigenous peoples of the country. Since the first arrival of Europeans, the Native peoples of Canada, like aboriginal groups elsewhere, have had their cultural heritage severely impacted by the imposition of foreign value systems and subsistence methods. It is only in very recent years that the larger society has recognized as legitimate the desire of indigenous peoples to retain their ancestral languages and traditions. In doing so it has also recognized that neocolonial approaches to schooling and training Native peoples have been ineffective at best and destructive at worst.

As a means of remedying the situation, one important step taken has been to place power and control over the education of Native children back into the hands of Native people (Alberta Education, Native Education Project 1985, Native Learning Resources Project 1985). This ensures that curriculum content not only includes concerns relevant to Native people, but also ensures that Native culture and history is presented from a Native point of view.

The information derived from archaeological research can make a meaningful contribution to our understanding of indigenous cultures, particularly in the realm of prehistory. Regrettably, many Native people in North America, particularly those in the United States, are generally ambivalent about the usefulness of archaeological research and indeed can be quite hostile to the approaches used by archaeologists. Unfortunately, archaeologists have largely failed to successfully communicate the benefits of archaeological research to the Native community. They have not only been reluctant to provide Natives a meaningful role in archaeological research, but have often ignored the concerns of Native peoples in the course of conducting research into sensitive areas of cultural life (Adams 1984, Cheek and Keel 1984, Ford 1984, Meighan 1984). Furthermore, archaeologists have failed to convince legislators to amend antiquities laws that place the rights of individual collectors and property owners over the collective rights of Native peoples and other citizens who wish to see their archaeological heritage protected in a substantive way.

The influence of the Native lobby over archaeology in education should not be ignored. In Canada, many provincial school systems are now ensuring that Native people have the final say over any curriculum content dealing with Native peoples—including content pertaining to Native prehistory. If archaeologists wish to have any influence over the inclusion of prehistoric archaeology content in school curricula and its treatment, they would be wise to ensure that they have the support of Native policy makers. Until Native concerns are addressed, archaeologists can expect to see the archaeology of indigenous peoples given short shrift in state or provincial curricula where Native people control curriculum content dealing with Native heritage. The result will be the exclusion of prehistory and the continued emphasis on the archaeology of ancient civilizations, perpetuating the destructive, treasure-hunting stereotypes so commonly associated with this archaeological specialty.

The Role of the Archaeologist in Archaeology Education

Despite the validity of many of the arguments supporting archaeology content in the curriculum, the vast majority of educators remain unconvinced. The reasons for this lack of success lie in the unwillingness of archaeologists to sponsor the kinds of programs which reflect the pedagogical goals and concerns of teachers, and their inability to communicate archaeological research in a manner accessible to the lay public.

In order to take advantage of curriculum openings that do exist, archaeologists must be prepared to make significant changes in how they traditionally interact with the school system, and also in the way they view the promotion of their discipline to the public.

THE NEEDS OF THE SCHOOL VERSUS THE NEEDS OF THE ARCHAEOLOGIST

For the most part, archaeologists' forays into the field of K-12 education are *ad hoc* at best—an occasional classroom visit, sporadic input into educational books and films, and infrequent provision of assistance to teachers planning archaeology projects. While many of these initiatives are successful in their own limited way, they are largely unsuccessful in a more substantive, long-term sense. They do not reinforce the notion of archaeology as a subject that is important to be studied, nor do they endeavor to use archaeology as a vehicle to explore core curricula (though see Messenger and Smith 1994 for Society for American Archaeology Public Education Committee activities).

This situation exists because most archaeologists do not share the same instructional goals as educators. Archaeologists tend to view school-based archaeology education solely as a means of achieving a narrowly defined, intrinsically self-serving, set of goals. The archaeologists' instructional agenda is primarily designed to perpetuate and protect archaeological research by ensuring a minimal amount of outside interference and a maximum amount of public support. The archaeological community is rarely interested in promoting the kinds of archaeology activities that satisfy the goals of education and reflect an understanding of educational theory and method. Otherwise we would have an abundance of field projects requiring student participation and a vast array of outreach materials from archaeological resource agencies detailing activities and resources suitable for the K-12 audience. Instead educators get a deluge of pamphlets and technical reports that confuse rather than enlighten, frustrate rather than help.

STUDENT FIELDWORK AND ARCHAEOLOGY

The strength of archaeology as a school subject lies in the intellectual, social, and physical demands it makes of the participants. Teachers have long recognized the strengths of archaeological excavation, for example, as a vehicle for teaching research skills, but continually encounter roadblocks when they attempt to find archaeological excavations which will accept their students as fieldworkers.

Archaeologists trundle out the same tired arguments against student participation in fieldwork. These include concerns about health and safety hazards, lack of care and precision in excavation, and lack of funding and time. Many of these arguments are simply a smoke screen to avoid the inconvenience of dealing with students.

The programs offered by facilities such as the Northwestern Field School at Kampsville, Illinois (Holm 1985), and the Toronto Board of Education Archaeology Unit (Smardz 1989) are the exception rather than the rule. If archaeologists were truly committed to archaeology in education they would make the policy changes necessary to foster student participation in archaeological fieldwork. An archaeological agency would more than fulfill its public relations requirements for the year if it devoted one contract excavation each year to student participation, and assigned an archaeologist to supervise that dig. Media support and corporate donations follow hard on the heels of innovative educational projects of this nature. The public education benefits are enormous.

Instructional Media and Archaeology

One major roadblock in the path of prehistoric archaeology in the schools is the perceived "dryness" of the topic. It is an unfortunate fact that teachers and students are excited by Classical and Mesoamerican archaeology and are largely disinterested in prehistory. Why this situation exists is debatable. One reason must surely be the "glitz factor"—the natural attraction people have for the "goodies" of Classical and Mesoamerican archaeology: the ruined temples, the gold, silver, and jade objects, sacred wells, and skeletal remains entombed in lava. As one junior high student bluntly informed me, "A few old buffalo bones aren't the Ark of the Covenant." Rightly or wrongly, teachers and students like hearing about mummies and doubloons and human sacrifices atop pyramids.

Publishers, in turn, have pandered to the public desire for "glitz" by producing coffee-table publications and educational textbooks which emphasize ancient civilizations. This trend, unfortunately, has persisted largely at the expense of prehistory. Curriculum writers discover that few suitable resources are listed for prehistory, but an abundance of publications dealing with ancient civilization *is* available. As a consequence the scope and sequence of any resulting curriculum will reflect an emphasis on civilization. When publishers subsequently discover that ancient civilization is listed in a new curriculum, they respond by producing *more* books on ancient civilization.

This unpleasant reality is not likely to change in the near future. If the archaeology community wants to ensure that prehistory is taught in schools, it must be prepared to accept the responsibility of producing educational materials themselves. This task is not as daunting as it may appear. The advances in computer technology have made desktop publishing a reality, and have consequently put small-scale publishing within the reach of agencies with modest budgets. Archaeological agencies can hire educators on a part-time or free-lance basis specifically to produce archaeology/prehistory materials for schools (as the U.S. Bureau of Land Management did in developing the "Intrigue of the Past" teacher's guide [Smith et al. 1993]). In fact, this alternative may prove to be the most suitable long-term solution to the problem of lack of prehistory materials.

In-house publishing, however, will not solve the image problem of prehistory. The public's preoccupation with "glitz" will subside only if archaeologists make the effort to present prehistory data in a manner accessible to the general public. The way to accomplish this is to produce materials specifically for the lay market which deemphasize statistical data and instead endeavor to recreate prehistoric life.

It is understandable that professional archaeologists are reluctant to sensationalize prehistory in order to put it on an equal footing with ancient civilization. Archaeologists are naturally squeamish about introducing any element to archaeological interpretation which might undermine the scientific aspects of archaeological research. Archaeologists also appear to dislike hypothesizing about human behavior in the distant past because human emotion and aesthetic sensibilities do not often manifest themselves in the archaeological record. But it is precisely the human element that draws people to archaeology and the human element that is missing from most archaeological portrayals of prehistory, with the possible exception of materials produced by the National Geographic Society. Surely there must be a way to make archaeology and prehistory more accessible to the lay audience, and in particular the school audience.

Dry-as-dust technical reports are simply not the answer, nor are generalized brochures that fail to interpret any archaeological topic in an in-depth way. While these publications may fulfil the archaeologist's scientific obligations, they do not satisfy the information needs of the general public or the school systems. Young audiences should also be considered when archaeologists participate in the development of museum galleries or interpretive centers dealing with archaeology and prehistory, which are often constructed with little thought given to the kinds of educational and interpretive programming most suited to archaeology and prehistory concepts. Suitable instructional approaches include narrative and role play for younger students, and experimental archaeology, simulated excavation, and laboratory activity for older students. Too often education officers are hired for a facility after construction and equipment purchase is completed, only to discover that the spaces set aside for educational purposes are inappropriate for the most useful kinds of activities. It is rare to have an education specialist actually involved in the architectural planning of a facility, but perhaps this is an idea worth considering.

It is time for archaeologists to collaborate with educators, media specialists, and writers to produce programs and materials that will attract the public. I am convinced that this can be achieved without compromising the archaeological data base.

Conclusion

Archaeologists must recognize that the survival of archaeology as a school topic lies in the willingness of the archaeological community to respond to the needs of the lay community. As professionals largely subsidized by public funds, archaeologists are accountable to the taxpayer, and are therefore not only responsible for investigating and protecting the archaeological resource base, but also for communicating effectively to the general public. For the most part, regulations and fines will not protect archaeological resources; an educated citizenry will. There is general agreement among educators and legislators that a comprehensive program of public education will often succeed in promoting positive social behaviors where punitive measures have failed. In order to get archaeology into schools, archaeologists must be prepared to respect the agenda of educators. To do so, they must become familiar with the current theoretical work being done in the educational specialties—e.g., environmental education, social studies, history, anthropology, Native studies, intercultural education, gifted education—which have a significant role to play in the future of archaeology education. They must also become familiar with instructional theory and method, and apply the principles of instructional design to the delivery of archaeology content.

Archaeologists should also encourage public educators to develop within the ranks of graduate schools of archaeology and anthropology. To accomplish this goal, students must be permitted to develop theoretical foundations outside of anthropology. They must be encouraged to produce scholarly work which may not always reflect the technical style of scholarly writing in archaeology (Fagan 1984:183). Most importantly, professional archaeologists must see this orientation as being as significant as a specialty in lithics, or faunal analysis, or any other area of archaeological work. Archaeology departments produce many graduates. Although the majority pursue careers in archaeology, some eventually function in educational capacities as museum curators, historic sites interpreters, and classroom teachers.

References Cited

Abell, R.P.
1985 Inference Making and Testing in a High School Archaeology Course. In *Archaeology and Education: A Successful Combination for Precollegiate Students*, edited by K.A. Holm and P.J. Higgins, pp. 45-49. Anthropology Curriculum Project, University of Georgia, Athens.

Adams, E.C.
1984 Archaeology and the Native American: A Case at Hopi. In *Ethics and Values in Archaeology*, edited by E. Green, pp. 236-242. The Free Press, Collier-Macmillan, New York.

Alberta Education, Native Education Project
1985 *Native Education in Alberta's Schools*. Alberta Education, Edmonton.

Calgary Board of Education
1989 *Environmental and Outdoor Education - Program of Studies and Teacher Resource Manual* (draft). Prepared for Alberta Education by the Calgary Board of Education. Copies available from the Alberta Department of Education, Edmonton.

Cheek, A.L., and B.C. Keel
1984 Value Conflicts in Osteo-Archaeology. In *Ethics and Values in Archaeology*, edited by E.L. Green, pp. 194-207. The Free Press, Collier-Macmillan, New York.

Dyche, B.
1985 Why Archaeology When Your Curriculum is Thinking Skills? Developing a Sequential Archaeological Curriculum for Grades 6 Through 12. In *Archaeology and Education: A Successful Combination for Precollegiate Students*, edited by K.A. Holm and P.J. Higgins, pp. 31-35. Anthropology Curriculum Project, University of Georgia, Athens.

Dyer, J.
1983 *Teaching Archaeology in Schools*. Shire Publications Ltd, Aylesbury.

Fagan, B.
1984 Archaeology and the Wider Audience. In *Ethics and Values in Archaeology*, edited by E.L. Green, pp. 175-183. The Free Press, Collier-Macmillan, New York.

Ford, R.I.
1984 Ethics and the Museum Archaeologist. In *Ethics and Values in Archaeology*, edited by E.L. Green, pp. 133-142. The Free Press, Collier-Macmillan, New York.

Hartman, D.W.
1985 Understanding Science Through Anthropological Enquiry: Two Cases. In *Archaeology and Education: A Successful Combination for Precollegiate Students*, edited by K.A. Holm and P.J. Higgins, pp. 51-66. Anthropology Curriculum Project, University of Georgia, Athens, Georgia.

Holm, K.A.
1985 Preparing Teachers to Introduce Archaeology Into the Curriculum. In *Archaeology and Education: A Successful Combination for Precollegiate Students*, edited by K.A. Holm and P.J. Higgins, pp. 51-66. Anthropology Curriculum Project, University of Georgia, Athens.

Kantrowitz, B., and P. Wingert
1989 How Kids Learn. *Newsweek*, April 17: 50-57.

Keen, M.J.
1988 Children Should Learn to Appreciate Science, Mathematics, and Technology in School. Shouldn't Scientists, Mathematicians and Technologists All Help? *Geoscience Canada* 15:281-282.

Meighan, C.W.
1984 Archaeology: Science or Sacrilege? In *Ethics and Values in Archaeology*, edited by E.L. Green, pp. 208-223. The Free Press, Collier-Macmillan, New York.

Messenger, P., and KC Smith (editors)
1994 *Archaeology and Public Education* vols. 4(3, 4) 5(1).

Native Learning Resources Project
1985 *Guidelines for the Development of Learning Resources*. Native Education Project, Alberta Department of Education, Edmonton.

Risinger, C.F.
1973 *The Dig: A Study in Archaeology*. Submitted to Social Science Education Consortium Inc., Boulder, CO. Copies available from ERIC Document Reproduction Service (No. ED 080 399).

Smardz, K.E.
1989 Toronto Students Dig Into Their Past! The Archaeological Resource Centre. *Teaching Anthropology Newsletter*, No. 14(Spring):2-8.

Smith, S.J., J.M. Moe, K.A. Letts, and D.M. Patterson
1993 *Intrigue of the Past: A Teacher's Activity Guide for Fourth through Seventh Grades.* U.S. Department of the Interior, Bureau of Land Management, Anasazi Heritage Center, Dolores, Colorado.

Wittich, W.A., and C.F. Schuller
1979 *Instructional Technology: Its Nature and Use.* 6th rev. ed. Harper & Row, New York.

Public Education through Public Media

Roy A. Gallant

The Public Trust Doctrine provides a unifying concept for the stewardship of archaeological resources. Selling the concept to the general public can best be achieved through the mass media. Positive approaches to working with the media are discussed and the public information component of the Center for the Study of the First Americans is briefly described.

An Indian, with fist raised to the heavens, sprinkles an offering of tobacco over the burials of his ancestors. He is not a Paleoindian but a living Native American named Robert Thomas. And, while his fist is raised in ceremonial offering, it is also raised in outrage over the wanton plundering of American Indian artifacts by commercial relic hunters who systematically destroy potential archaeological sites and further deplete the store of these objects. An estimated 70 percent of artifacts recovered to date—from all Indian sites in North America—are in the hands of private collectors and virtually useless to scholars because they lack documentation.

The scene just mentioned occurred at Slack Farm in western Kentucky, where in 1987 ten relic collectors, treasure seekers, looters, grave robbers—whatever you choose to call them—left some 450 craters in their desecration of at least 650 grave sites of a 40-acre Indian burial ground. The site dates from about 200 B.C. to A.D. 1650. The diggers had paid the landowner $10,000 for the privilege of excavating over a few months. A 500-year-old human effigy pipe from the site brought $4,500.

When law officers investigating the dig discovered countless human jawbones, leg bones, finger bones, and human teeth strewn among the craters, they stopped the digging and charged the ten with "desecration of a venerated object," a misdemeanor punishable by a maximum fine of $500 and up to one year in jail. Four of the ten looters lived in Illinois or Indiana and could not be extradited for a misdemeanor. In

March 1988, the Kentucky Legislature upgraded the crime to a felony, which does permit extradition. However, Indiana failed to pass such legislation, so grave looters in that state continue to be prosecuted only for trespassing, a misdemeanor carrying a fine as low as one dollar. A detailed report of the Slack Farm incident appeared in *National Geographic* magazine (Arden 1989:376-393).

The question all of this raises is "Who should own our past?"

At present, in the absence of federal regulation of archaeological resources not subject to federal land management, "most archaeological sites on private land have no legal protection from destruction, [which means that about] two-thirds of the United States is open to unregulated collecting, site destruction, or both," according to archaeologist Ruthann Knudson (1989:72) writing in the January/February issue of *Archaeology* magazine.

As other presenters have made clear, "Archaeology is not just for archaeologists . . . archaeological resources are part of a public trust" (Knudson, this volume). That notion may be new to at least some archaeologists—and some may not be entirely comfortable with it. It is virtually unknown to most outside the archaeological community, including many journalists and educators.

Writing in the *Michigan Law Review*, Joseph L. Sax said that "there are certain interests that are intrinsically so important to every citizen that their free availability tends to mark the society as one of citizens rather than serfs; to protect these, it is necessary to be especially wary so no individual or group acquires power to control them" (Sax 1970). Knudson (this volume) amplifies that thought when she says, "each government or private individual with legal jurisdiction over the physical context of archaeological deposits has a trust responsibility to protect the joint ownership rights of the entire human community."

Reaching the Public

Those of us involved in professional archaeology, either directly as investigators or indirectly through affiliation with archaeological organizations such as the Center for the Study of the First Americans (CSFA) or as educators in the classroom, bear the responsibility to communicate to the public the significance of our work and its relevance to the acquisition of knowledge of our collective heritage. Educating the public through museums and the media is our best hope of achieving that goal. How then do we reach the public through the mass media of communication, and when we do, what do we say?

In the papers we write and lectures we give, and in interviews with journalists of print and electronic media, there are several attitudes and messages we can and should convey to present a united front for the common good of archaeology. There is public interest in archaeology and most journalists whose beat is the scientific community are eager to find fresh accounts and viewpoints about the peopling of the Americas. Those who may doubt such a public interest need only read the *Natural History* magazine series of more than a dozen articles published in 1986, 1987, and 1988, written by Stanford, Guidon, Haynes, Turner, Adovasio, and others. In a larger context, *National Geographic* magazine, *Newsweek*, *Omni*, *Discover*, *Time*, and other publications routinely print major articles probing our human origins and hominid evolution, not to mention a number of popular books by Coe, Kopper, *Readers Digest*, Pfeiffer, and one of my own.

Articles in all such publications nearly always are based on interviews of experts, and there is our opportunity to join as one voice and broadcast the importance of all archaeological research that bears on the peopling of the Americas. When you are interviewed by a local television station or by a science journalist from the print media, take that opportunity to stress that archaeological resources are part of a public trust owned by the members of the human world community. While some may consider that concept premature in the context of current domestic and international politics, it is, nevertheless, a notion that all of us gathered at this World Summit share and should be advocating at every opportunity.

To date, such views have not always been characterized by coherency among us. An immovable late arrivalist—one who favors the first migrations to the Americas as occurring not much before 13,000 years before the present—should not be expected to beat the drum of an early arrivalist—one who favors a date of 40,000 or more years before the present. But if you want to take a colleague to task, do it in a professional journal where your readers are knowledgeable enough to follow your argument. When appearing before the public a more cautious and gentler stance is advisable, such as that taken by late arrivalist Paul Martin in his *Natural History* magazine article in which he challenged in the public eye the dates of several sites, including the Koch mastodon site, points from Sandia Cave, the Holly Oak pendant, and Smith Creek Cave. "Let the inevitable burst of hype dissipate," he advised, "while the evidence is reviewed calmly, preferably in place and ideally by skeptics (Martin 1987:13)."

Take a Positive Approach

The image of an open-minded investigator who is not about to skin anyone who disagrees with him is the surest and quickest way to win the respect of the science writer chronicling your story, and the confidence of those reading the story or watching you being interviewed on television.

This is not to say that there should not be disagreement among investigators. Disagreement is inevitable, and its value to science should be made known to the public. Disagreement over the presumed validity or interpretation of data is what provides science with its vigor and helps characterize science as a viable search for truth. But malice and acrimony are the surest means to arouse the public's suspicion and distaste for science and scientists. With the deplorable state of scientific literacy in the United States today we must do whatever we can to help generate respect and admiration for our work rather than suspicion and hostility.

Perhaps more than any other institution, the CSFA has as one of its major purposes to bring to the academic community, as well as the public, current findings and ideas about the peopling of the Americas. One of our goals is to be *the* resource center for educational and mass market publishers who want information about the peopling of the Americas. This World Summit is bound to provide us with significant thrust toward that goal. For example, many of you have agreed to let the Center photograph artifacts from your collections and to make those photographs part of the Center's photographic library which will soon be in a position to supply the technical and popular press with thousands of photographs of archaeological sites, investigators in the field, and numerous artifacts that otherwise would lie in secret in specimen drawers. So we encourage you to make use of our abilities as communicators and educators, and to make it known during your associations with the media that we exist and are eager to offer our services.

References Cited

Arden, H.
1989 Who Owns the Past? *National Geographic* 175:376-392.

Knudson, R.
1989 North America's Threatened Heritage. *Archaeology* 42:71-73, 106.

Martin. P.S.
1987 The First Americans: Clovisia the Beautiful. *Natural History* 96:10-13.

Sax, J.L.
1970 The Public Trust Doctrine in Natural Resources Law: Effective Judicial Intervention. *Michigan Law Review* 68:471-566.

Public-Private Partnerships in Archaeology

Judith A. Bense

Our generation faces the fact that archaeological resources are being destroyed at an alarming rate and could well be largely eliminated in the span of our careers. We are in the same position as the environmentalists of thirty years ago who realized that the entire country's water, soil, and air were being polluted at an alarming rate. The red flags are up for archaeology and we must develop methods that affect the roots of the problem: economic justification of archaeology, public education, and new funding sources.

Market Strategy

A few professionals, especially McGimsey and Davis (1974), realized twenty years ago that site destruction was getting out of control and were instrumental in developing laws to protect archaeological sites on federal property and areas to be impacted by federally funded projects in the United States. Those laws and regulations are still being refined and, despite problems with enforcement, hundred of thousands of sites are now being protected. However, we are quickly realizing that this is only the beginning of the solution. Two-thirds of the land in the United States is not federally but privately owned and most of the projects which impact archaeological sites are not federally funded. This is especially true for the major growth areas in the United States, particularly in the north and southeast.

Florida is the fastest-growing state in the nation with 30,000 immigrants monthly. Because of this growth, all forms of development have been impacting the archaeological sites in Florida. The vast majority of sites fall through the federal and state safety nets, since most development is funded privately or with bond money and most development projects are on private property. Little can be done under current law to protect most archaeological sites in the way of development. New methods of archaeological resource management are being developed in Florida in response to this onslaught. Some of these programs have been very successful and are serving as models for other developing areas.

Presently, northwest Florida is not as over developed as are many places in central and south Florida. The archaeological resources west of Tallahassee are well preserved, but are threatened as development encroaches at a ever-increasing rate. In order to deal with this deteriorating situation, we in northwest Florida have taken an approach which emphasizes marketing and developing archaeology in the private sector. We have approached the protection and conservation of archaeological resources located on private property in a new light, emphasizing their value for the people and community who own them. Through marketing and developing archaeology, we build partnerships to develop, save, and share archaeological sites in northwest Florida. This approach has generated support for and interest in archaeology by the private sector, municipalities, and the state. This paper will present a brief overview of some of these partnerships.

Harnessing Power

The first example of such a partnership involved the electric utility for northwest Florida, the Gulf Power Company. In 1984, this company was planning to build a $25 million corporate headquarters on the Pensacola bayfront. The proposed location was archaeologically sensitive as it had been a Creole neighborhood for 150 years, it was in the vicinity of a colonial governor's villa, and a few prehistoric sherds had been recovered there over the years. A check with the state determined that there was no federal or state archaeological compliance required for the project. Consequently, a small delegation of concerned professionals approached the utility company with an unsolicited proposal to test the 11-acre parcel to determine if there were any significant archaeological deposits present. Testing, which cost approximately $17,000, identified two significant archaeological deposits: a sealed single component Early Woodland village with scores of refuse pits, and the undisturbed deposits of the entire 150 years of the Creole residential neighborhood.

These archaeological resources were evaluated first in terms of their potential to meet Gulf Power's needs. The value of the sites to science was of primary importance to archaeologists, but not to the utility company. But Gulf Power had both short- and long-term public relations problems. The company had been receiving negative publicity about the construction of the corporate headquarters due to the building's excessive cost, customers' perceived lack of need for the new facility, and the necessary relocation of an entire African-American neighborhood from the building site. The company also had chronic public relations problems because of acid-rain pollution and its monopoly on electricity rates. Consequently, a proposal was developed that focused on how the company could develop the archaeological resources on its property into a high-profile positive public relations project which made a significant contribution to the community at large. This contribution consisted of several educational products, including a book for general readers and an archaeology teaching unit for the public schools comprising a videotape documentary, slide-tape documentary, bulletin board, replicated artifacts, and a coloring book. An accessible public exhibit of the archaeology was proposed for the lobby of the new building. The proposed project included a ground-breaking ceremony, ribbon cutting, and a VIP tour of the exhibit. A stylish logo was proposed for the project which could be used on coffee cups, shirts, power bill inserts, and the like. The project was given the catchy name "Hawkshaw" after the African-American neighborhood which would be virtually removed by the project.

The proposal was immediately approved by Gulf Power Company and was successful. The company subsequently was awarded the first Department of the Interior National Public Service Award for archaeology given to a private energy company, as well as the top state public relations "Golden Image" award. Archaeology was able to give the company what nothing else could: reams of positive newspaper coverage, TV spots, and editorials all over the Southeast. Through archaeology, Gulf Power could do something good for the community and for science and be proud of the extent of its commitment. Today, Hawkshaw symbolizes the living past which would have been forgotten and destroyed if Gulf Power had not preserved the past as it built for the future. This successful project set the stage for marketing archaeology to the private sector.

Capturing the City Fathers (and Mothers)

The next partnership to be developed in the Pensacola area was with the city. Pensacola was originally a colonial town; it is the site of the oldest European settlement attempt in the United States (AD 1559) and has been continuously occupied since 1690. Many of the significant colonial archaeological deposits have been destroyed by nonfederally funded redevelopment projects as well as by avid bottle collecting and amateur digging. In order to control the destruction of archaeological sites in the city, a compliance system was developed that is a local version of the federal requirements for compliance with Section 106 of the National Historic Preservation Act. A large and vocal political action committee was formed which proposed to the city council that it initiate an archaeological review procedure on city-owned property. This would put council members in a leadership role and assure that large city-sponsored projects would no longer destroy the city's archaeological resources. (For more detailed information on the development and contents of this archaeological review resolution in Pensacola see Bense [1987].)

The proposal was passed unanimously in 1985, and since then a series of archaeological projects has been conducted in compliance with it. The most frequent type of project is street and utility renovation in the historic district. The resolution was strengthened within two years of passage to include private companies that conduct subsurface work in city rights-of-way. The expanded coverage resulted in monitoring of extensive trenching for fiber-optic cable installations throughout the archaeologically sensitive areas of the city. In addition, an archaeological survey of city-owned lands was performed that served as a basis for developing an archaeological management plan for the city.

While the archaeological review resolution is an important element in the conservation of Pensacola's archaeological resources, we have discovered that it is not high on the list of priorities of the city staff targeted to implement it. However, the public is now much more aware of the location of the archaeologically sensitive areas in the city, and we have found that the "watch dogs" in the local archaeological society and an educated public are the true enforcers of the resolution.

How the Partnership Works: The Fort of Pensacola Example

Among the seemingly constant stream of municipal construction projects in the historic old city area, a large utility and streetscape improvement project covering several blocks was designed in the late 1980s. This particular project crossed through the colonial fort area of Pensacola. Plans called for massive new utilities, street surfaces, street lights, sidewalks, and the planting of scores of large trees. In addition, many of the existing buried utilities were to be removed and replaced by new lines in deep trenches. In late fall 1989, a compliance plan (Bense 1989a) was developed in accordance with the city archaeological review policy. It began with a modest budget to cover testing of several sidewalk areas and the evaluation of several areas of significant deposits to be impacted by construction. Subsequently a modest budget proposal was developed for mitigation of the project. Mitigation was to be accomplished primarily by recording data and recovering material during archaeological monitoring of utility-trench excavation and construction.

On the second day of construction in 1990, as the asphalt was being removed in an area thought to have been disturbed by earlier utility trenches, an eighteenth-century British field cannon was discovered. Members of the press had been notified and were present as the cannon was hoisted from the street to the neighboring state museum. With the cameras rolling, workers in an adjacent area removing more pavement exposed foundations from a colonial period building (1752-1821). This discovery created a second story for the press: the Fort of Pensacola. This became the largest archaeological event in Pensacola's history. As more and more of the fort was exposed in the street, public interest grew. Finally, remnants of the sentry house, as well as interior structures built by the British in the late 1760s in the main gate area, were exposed and documented. This fort gate is the very one through which, in 1821, Andrew Jackson walked to accept U.S. possession of Florida from Spain. Here Old Hickory raised the first official U.S. flag over Florida.

This project was in the heart of Pensacola, in the street, right next to a city park and at the foot of the largest museum in the historic district, where public accessibility was excellent. Hundreds of people came daily to watch this 200-year-old piece of U.S. history brought into the late twentieth century. People wanted maps that would show them how the remnants of the old fort fit into today's environment. They were excited and eager to sign petitions to save the fort and develop it into a first-class outdoor archaeological exhibit.

The media took to the story, giving it extensive local coverage which grew into a national story covered on ABC's *Good Morning America* and twice on CNN television. A "fort watch" was held by a large regional newspaper, including one Sunday front-page story with color drawings and pictures that covered almost the entire page. In addition, several editorials appeared in the paper during the project. Wire-service articles were also picked up by papers throughout the state and most of the Southeast region. This made the Colonial Fort of Pensacola very well known. Regular tours of the area were incorporated into the public tours of the historic area. Area schools made field trips to the site with increasing frequency. Tourists, especially from the northern United States, began to visit the site and the tourist information center began to pinpoint the site as "the" spot to visit. Museums and commercial establishments surrounding the site had record visitation and receipts in February 1990, and the adjacent city park was a popular "archaeology lunch" spot.

The public and press were immediately concerned that the city would destroy the fort and the foundations of its buildings by putting the large planned storm-water main right through it and paving over the rest of it. A petition by the Pensacola Archaeological Society circulated to protect the site, excavate, and develop it into an upscale outdoor archaeology exhibit. The Historic Pensacola Preservation Board immediately put the cannon on display on the steps of the museum and pressed hard for closing the street.

The city's dilemma ended with a typical negotiation between the members of the archaeology partnership that had been developed in Pensacola between university archaeologists, city staff, avocational support groups, and the public. Each partner had a range of priorities within which a plan could be acceptable; however, for the first time in Pensacola, the most powerful partner was now the public. The city knew that if the site was destroyed there would be a public outcry. It felt pressure to keep the street open, but had to avoid further impacting the site by moving parking facilities to the far side of the right-of-way. The Preservation Board and staff requested additional budget funds from the state for the excavation and exhibit of the site. The press kept the pressure on.

The fact that the fort was discovered in response to the city's archaeological review policy put a white hat squarely on the city council; however, it also put the responsibility of stewardship on their shoulders. The initial mitigation estimate had jumped and the construction budget for the municipal bond-funded project had no funds allocated for archaeology. Seizing the opportunity to take the lead, the university president met with the city manager as chief executive officers of organizations with a mutual interest in the problem, and were able to develop a plan of action.

Funds were allocated by the city for site mitigation with a commitment from the university and the Pensacola Historic Preservation Board to raise the funds needed for site excavation and development. The compromise plan was a city-funded program to document and recover a sample of the colonial features. The street design was changed to a serpentine pattern around the intact archaeological deposits, and the utility trench was placed across the street. The city provided sturdy filter cloth to cover the archaeological site, and two feet of fill to buffer the site from impacts.

The now well-organized and popular Pensacola Archaeological Society and experienced university archaeology students provided free trained labor; through this volunteer effort the city's mitigation costs were reduced by at least 65 percent. The archaeological society also provided a popular information table for the public, which gave out handouts about the project, sold commemorative T-shirts, and provided one-on-one information. As a result of the volunteer support, the only paid staff for the entire archaeological testing and mitigation effort were three supervisors and a public tour guide.

Everyone came out a winner as well as a paying partner in this project. University archaeologists recovered priceless information and protected nationally significant deposits. The city looked good because it had the leadership to have archaeologists on the job when the construction took place and because it paid its way. During the initial discovery phase, the Historic Preservation Board took the lead in initiating the large funding request, providing historical information, and exhibiting the main artifact, the cannon. The archaeological society provided labor, telephone trees, and an information table, and gained scores of new members. The media had a field day and reporters had bylines and feature stories for several weeks. This is how it works in Pensacola. We handle it one project at a time, giving each partner respect yet demanding that each shoulders its responsibility.

After the dust had settled, with the most significant archaeological areas in the street right-of-way protected, we designed a public archaeology project to literally "develop" the colonial military features that had caught public attention. The Fort of Pensacola Colonial Archaeological Train was developed, a series of five outdoor exhibits and a significant area inside the museum which itself today sits inside the former colonial fort. Public support was generated for two state grants of almost a half-million dollars to conduct intensive archaeological research and exhibit design and installation. The public will be able to view real archaeological features from colonial Pensacola from boardwalks elevated over building foundations, outdoor cooking ovens, and refuse pits. The discovery of the cannon in the street is recreated in a museum room where the actual cannon is embedded in a reconstructed street construction scene.

The Bottom Line

Archaeology is now alive and well in Pensacola because concerned residents realized that it was up to them to find a way to stop the irreversible destruction of our archaeological resources. Pensacola is not an especially rich, poor, big, or small city. The residents here represent the full spectrum of U.S. citizens. A partnership approach can be developed among the key players in any town. The essential ingredient is acceptance of responsibility by the archaeological community, both professional and amateur, to ensure that something be done to stop the destruction and neglect of nonrenewable archaeological resources. It is possible to mainstream archaeology. The long suit in all this is that the public already has a natural interest in archaeology and, once educated and involved in it, has the power to make changes. This is the key to the growing strength of Pensacola archaeology. Now almost all of the 250,000 people living here know that there is archaeology in Pensacola and that it is a valuable community resource. It can be managed just like other resources, such as water, runoff, or air quality. Now is the time to start this kind of local involvement across the nation. Without grassroots support, too many archaeological sites will be gone and we will leave a poorer and needlessly depleted legacy for future generations.

These concepts of marketing and developing functional partnerships work because of the public interest and media appeal of archaeology. Archaeology has something to sell and it has tangible products that people like. The private sector and the business people that operate local government are used to marketing and relate well to this strategy. The marketing approach to archaeology has caused the program at the moderate-sized, regional University of West Florida to grow dramatically ever since we began employing it. Archaeology is good for the university because through it the mission of community service is met in a direct and high-profile manner. The university is pleased at the consistently increasing publicity archaeology has brought to the institution, including regular local and media coverage, exposure on the international program, "CNN Science," and articles in popular public magazines such as *Southern Living*. Selling archaeology to the private sector and local government is not difficult. In fact, it is easier than selling it to the federal government or the National Science Foundation, the traditional source of archaeological research funding in the United States.

The latest advancement in the Pensacola public-private partnerships in archaeology is the formation of a committee of men and women from the business community, civic leaders, and fund raisers dedicated to enhancing Pensacola archaeology. These individuals realize the importance of the university's academic archaeology program to the development of community archaeology for the local and touring public. They realize that the public likes archaeology and that Pensacola has excellent resources in easily accessible areas. While millions of people visit the northern Gulf Coast each year, Pensacola's tourism figures are relatively low. Increasing tourism through the development of Pensacola's archaeological resources is an appealing concept to this committee, and its members understand that enhancing the local academic program is one of the keys to that develoment. They also understand that development of archaeology will take money and political support, and they are organized to obtain both. This committee is literally mainstreaming archaeology in Pensacola. It is through groups such as this that academic-public-private partnerships are fostered and that archaeological sites are considered a valuable resources to be saved much like clean beaches, air, and water resources. Unrestricted development can get out of control, but the archaeology partners in development projects can and do preserve the resources.

Although there is a long way to go, Pensacola's archaeological resources are much better protected than they were a decade ago, and this has only been made possible through the development of partnerships. Archaeologists cannot continue to work only with colleagues in quiet scholarship and expect the resource to last. Because destruction is constant, we must take some of our time to be good partners to the resource that cannot speak for itself: the sites.

References Cited

Bense, J.A.
1987 Development of a Management System for Archaeological Resources in Pensacola, Florida. In *Living in Cities: Current Research in Urban Archaeology*. Special Publication Series, Number 5.

1989a The Pensacola Archaeological Preservation Compliance Plan. Report on file with the Pensacola City Council.

1989b *The Pensacola Archaeological Survey, Technical Report*, Volumes I and II. Pensacola Archaeological Society Publication Number 1. Pensacola, Florida.

McGimsey, C.R., III, and H.A. Davis
1974 *The Management of Archaeological Resources*. Airlie House Report. Special Publication of the Society for American Archaeology, Washington.

VI. Funding

Funding archaeological endeavors is a critical matter, perhaps even more important than the legal constraints with which we must abide and the procedural requirements we must satisfy. Indeed, adequate funding is one of the criteria to be satisfied in obtaining a permit to excavate a site for research purposes on U.S. federal and state lands. The papers contained in this section review financial support for First Americans research by the major U.S. government granting agencies (Watson) and provide guidance on how to tap the private sector (Williams) and information helpful in approaching the major U.S. land-managing agencies (Douglas). All three of these funding sources are critical to studying and managing First Americans archaeological and paleo- environmental resources.

The amount of money spent by the U.S. government, and the expenses incurred by the private sector because of U.S. heritage protection requirements, have been of great interest over the past few years. Estimates have ranged from the tens of millions of dollars to as high as $200 million or more annually. The precise amount spent in a given year is impossible to ascertain, and even an estimated amount is difficult to determine because of the various record-keeping practices employed by different federal agencies and the legal impossibility of requiring the private sector to report the actual costs of archaeological resource management. These operational costs are proprietary information closely guarded from the competition. Consequently, archaeological expenditures may appear to be significant, or insignificant, depending on the circumstances.

It is even more difficult to ascertain the amount of funds spent on First Americans resource research and conservation. Yet understanding what funds are available for such research and conservation, and how they are allocated and reported, is essential to implement First Americans-related programs.

In the United States, the Moss-Bennett Act of 1974 (Archeological and Historic Preservation Act) and the Archaeological Resources Protection Act (ARPA) of 1979 require that the Secretary of the Interior annually report to Congress the cost and effectiveness of both acts. Until fiscal year 1985, a comprehensive and accurate accounting of federal agency programs under these laws was impossible because of bureaucratic inertia and/or accounting practices. However, a series of events created an awareness that it was in the best interest of U.S. federal archaeologists to assure that more accurate information was available to the Congress. Among the events that caught the attention of the Congress and the federal administration were several audits conducted by the U.S. General Accounting Office that were critical of the federal archaeology program. Especially important was the finding that agencies were not providing information on the program to the Secretary of the Interior. Since 1985, a database has been developing that quantifies most of the federal archaeology program activities, including the related costs (Keel et al. 1989, McManamon et al. 1993).

Despite the current perception in the United States of a shortage of funds for desirable archaeological projects, it is appropriate to look back at least briefly to the period prior to the enactment of the National Historic Preservation Act (1966), the Moss-Bennett Act, and ARPA. Between 1956 and 1986, reported federal expenditures for archaeology increased exponentially. In 1956, all federal rescue archaeology was conducted by the River Basin Surveys (RBS), a unit of the Bureau of American Ethnology within the Smithsonian Institution. Although administratively housed in the Smithsonian, the RBS was funded by annual transfers of funds appropriated by Congress to the National Park Service. During fiscal year 1956, RBS cooperatively assisted colleges, universities, and museums to carry out 25 data recovery expeditions and five survey projects for a total of approximately $123,000. These projects were carried out in reservoir areas by the U.S. Corps of Engineers and the Bureau of Reclamation. In 1986, the Corps reported that $21 million has been spent by the Corps or its land-use applicants for archaeology, and the Bureau reported that over $7 million had been similarly spent (Keel et al. 1989).

Again, it is impossible to separate out First Americans-related activities, but probably no more than five percent, and perhaps not even as much as one percent, of the federal archaeology program affects First Americans resources. However, even one percent of the funds expended to support the program equals if not exceeds the research funds available for First Americans research through the sources described by Watson.

Bennie C. Keel
Ruthann Knudson

References Cited

Keel, B.C., F.P. McManamon, and G.S. Smith (compilers)
1989 *Federal Archeology: The Current Program. Annual Report to Congress on the Federal Archeological Program FY 1985 and FY 1986.* U.S. Department of the Interior, National Park Service, Washington.

McManamon, F.P., P.C. Knoll, R. Knudson, G.S. Smith, and R.C. Waldbauer (compilers)
1993 *Federal Archeological Programs and Activities.* U.S. Department of the Interior, National Park Service, Archeological Assistance, Departmental Consulting Archeologist, Washington.

Federal U.S. Funding: First Americans Research

Patty Jo Watson

The majority of U. S. federal funding for First Americans grant research comes from the National Science Foundation (NSF). The National Endowment for the Humanities, the National Institutes of Health, the U.S. Public Health Service, and the Smithsonian Institution are also sources of research funds. In the 1980s, despite modest appropriation increases to NSF, real available dollars were slightly below the 1978 level. Examples of grants made over the past 20 years demonstrate the variety of research undertaken with federal funds.

The majority of federal U.S. funding for scientific research on topics, sites, and regions relevant to the peopling of the Americas has come from the National Science Foundation (NSF). A large array of general environmental, paleoenvironmental, and biological research potentially relevant to that topic is not addressed here; I focus on relatively direct research funding. The Anthropology Program of NSF awards the majority of such funds, although support for interdisciplinary projects sometimes comes from other NSF programs, such as Climate Dynamics, Geochemistry, or Environmental Geosciences. The Anthropology Program awards $5 to $7 million per year for basic research in archaeology, cultural anthropology, and physical anthropology. John Yellen, program director for archaeology, kindly made available to me the annual grant lists of the Anthropology Program for 1978 to 1987 (NSF 1987) and 1990, 1991, and 1994 (NSF 1994). These lists are the source of much of the detail included in the following overview.

The Anthropology Program budget in 1989 was $7.2 million, of which approximately $2.7 million went to archaeology (38 percent). To judge from the 1978-87 data, that figure is fairly representative; $2 to $3 million per year go directly to archaeological excavation and analysis (including dating) and for curation of archaeological collections. NSF archaeology expenditures in the 1990s were $3.2 million in 1992, $3.3 million in 1993, and $3.5 million in 1994. Research on topics relevant to the peopling of the Americas is approximately six percent of the total expended on archaeology. These sums range from doctoral dissertation grants of a few thousand dollars to multiyear, multidisciplinary, multi-tens-of-thousands-of-dollars grants to senior researchers.

NSF money for individual or team-directed projects on the peopling of the Americas pays for basic data collection in the field, for analysis of all sorts, including dating, and sometimes for prepublication expenses as well. Besides increasing knowledge of Pleistocene-Early Holocene archaeology, these funds subsidize graduate training and career development of individual scholars devoted to Paleoindian and other relevant research.

Examples of 1980s and 1990s U.S. doctoral dissertation projects relevant to the peopling of the Americas include:

• Interassemblage variability in the El Inga region, highland Ecuador;

• Amino acid racemization dating in northern California;

• Bison procurement in Northern Plains prehistory;

• Paleo-Indian technological organization and settlement mobility in the Great Lakes;

• Haystack Cave: A methodological case study for evaluating Late Pleistocene cave deposits;

• Paleo-Indian research in the alkali basin, central Oregon;

• Stable isotope analysis of paleosols;

• Archaeological analysis of bone;

• Bone density and bone bed structure at Mill Iron, Montana; and

• A dynamic view of Paleoindian assemblages at the Hell Gap site, Wyoming: reconstructing lithic technological systems.

NSF dissertation grants had a ceiling of $10,000 until the limit was raised to $12,000 in 1989. The grants just listed ranged from $5,635 to $11,624.

Examples of senior proposals funded by NSF during the 1980s for research relevant to the peopling of the Americas are:

• Cultural adaptation to ecological change on the Llano Estacado ($87,000);

• Analysis of the Agate Basin type site materials ($8,404);

• Excavations at Little Salt Spring, Florida ($33,683);

• Munsungun Lake archaeological research project ($152,275);

• Archaeology of the Dietz Clovis site, central Oregon ($49;992);

• Monte Verde: an early settlement in Chile ($69,401);

• Early human adaptation to Andean South America;

• Settlement around a former freshwater lake at Punta Negra ($47,208); and

• Archaeological excavation of Danger Cave ($68,625).

NSF has other categories of support beside that for predoctoral and postdoctoral archaeological excavation and analysis. Those of most concern here I have lumped under the heading of Paleoenvironment and Archaeometry. Examples of such research include:

• Late Quaternary Geochronology ($20,000, plus $4,761 from the Environmental Geosciences program);

• The Accuracy of Radiocarbon and Amino Acid Racemization Dating of Pleistocene Age Bone ($140,695);

• Radiocarbon Dating of Bone Apatite—a New Approach ($35,568);

• Workshop on Calibration of the Radiocarbon Time Scale ($118,237);

• Improvements in Radiocarbon Dating at the UCR Laboratory ($155,835);

• Radiocarbon Dating Laboratories Core Support ($234,245);

• Support of a Radiocarbon Dating Facility ($157,706);

• Radiocarbon Dating of Amino Acid Components of Bone Using Accelerator Mass Spectrometry ($119,976);

• Alaska Tephrochronology Project ($39,770);

• Seasonal Mortality and Life History of Pleistocene Mastodonts and Mammoths ($50,000 from Anthropology and $49,000 from Systematic Biology);

• NSF Accelerator Facility for Radioisotope Analysis ($147,000 from Anthropology, $25,000 each from Chemical Oceanography, Marine Geology and Geophysics, and Oceanographic Technology);

• Radiocarbon Dating of Individual Amino Acids in Fossil Bone by Accelerator Mass Spectrometry ($27,820);

- Phytolith analysis in archaeology ($155,238);
- Dietary reconstruction with stable isotopes ($202,119);
- Isotopic composition of paleosol carbonates and organic matter ($78,400);
- Human interaction with North American Pleistocene Proboscideans (>$28,126);
- Clovis-Folsom-Plainview geochronology, climate change, and the Pleistocene-Holocene transition (>$25,761); and
- Barium in bone as a paleodietary indicator (>$97,353).

The NSF supports Arctic science, engineering, and education, primarily through its Office of Polar Programs. Fiscal year 1993 grants supporting Paleoindian or Paleoindian-related studies include:

- Late Cenozoic history of the Bering Sea ($142,263);
- Late Quaternary environments and climate change in the eastern Canadian Arctic reconstructed from lake sediment cores ($15,088);
- Paleoclimatic significance of major high latitude post-glacial tephra eruptions in Alaska and Siberia ($45,167);
- Chronostratigraphy of Pleistocene high-sea-level and glacial deposits, northeastern Bristol Bay, Alaska ($44,644);
- Workshop on the role of the Laurentide ice sheet in the climate system ($20,208);
- Paleoenvironments of the Bering land bridge at the end of the last glaciation ($63,846);
- Human performance and adaptation in polar environments ($45,069);
- The Arctic LTER project: Terrestrial and freshwater research on ecological controls ($1,204,098);
- The chronology and ecology of post-glacial colonization of the Americas ($24,964);
- Late Quaternary climate change in the eastern interior of Alaska: A multidisciplinary pilot study ($113,509); and
- A heirarchic GIS for studies of process, pattern, and scale in Arctic ecosystems ($67,542).

The NSF Anthropology Program also provides funds for curating large and/or important collections through its Systematic Research Collections Awards. Moreover, at least once in the past twenty years, NSF Anthropology paid the travel expenses of U.S. scientists to a major conference, the 11th Congress of the International Association for Quaternary Research that met in Moscow in 1982. In 1994, NSF supported computerization of the MesoAmerican and South American Archaeological collections of the Peabody Museum of Natural History, Yale.

Although NSF provides the lion's share of basic federal funding for archaeological field and laboratory research on peopling of the Americas topics, a few other federal agencies or institutions also contribute support. A few archaeological surveys that identified First Americans resources were funded by the National Endowment for the Humanities from 1966 to the present time (NEH 1994), as well as publication of data from the Ayacucho site of Peru. And now that some kinds of genetic studies can be carried out on prehistoric materials, National Institutes of Health (NIH) and the U.S. Public Health Service (PHS) provide occasional support as well.

The Smithsonian Institution's large and—for the United States—venerable anthropological and biological collections are, of course, a very valuable scholarly resource for peopling of the Americas and a wide variety of other research topics. Furthermore, until recently the Smithsonian Institution's Radiation Biology Laboratory sometimes provided radiocarbon dates to excavators of sites containing early materials. For example, most of the dates for Meadowcroft, and some of those for Lautaro Nunez's Paleoindian sites in northern Chile came from the Smithsonian laboratory. The move of that laboratory a few years ago from the Smithsonian to the University of Pittsburgh was partially funded by a 1987 NSF grant.

Summary

The bulk of federal funding for archaeological, archaeometric, and paleoenvironmental research specifically directed toward the peopling of the Americas has come from the Anthropology Program of the NSF, and totals several tens of thousands to a few hundred thousand dollars per year. Direct financial aid is also available, for some projects, from two other major funding agencies: the National Endowment for the Humanities and the NIH. The Smithsonian Institution, although not a funding agency like the other three, played a vital role in late nineteenth and early twentieth century research on the peopling of the Americas (Meltzer 1994), and is an excellent scholarly resource at present for all manner of research on the peoples of the Americas.

Although the implication is present throughout this account, I conclude by stating explicitly that if you pay taxes in the United States you have a palpable financial stake in this research; you are quite literally a patron of it. I hope and believe you should derive considerable satisfaction and pride from that fact.

As to federal funding in the near future, that question can be best addressed by simply noting that the NSF Anthropology budget has increased relatively little between 1978, when it was about $5.4 million, to 1989 when it was $7.2 million. Considering national and international rates of inflation during that period, a $1.8 million raise in ten years represents an actual loss in research money buying power. Hence, substantial increases in the NSF Anthropology budget are necessary if cutting-edge research on peopling of the Americas is to be initiated and maintained at adequate levels over the next decade. Therefore, we taxpayers who value modern interdisciplinary archaeological research in general and research on peopling of the Americas in particular should take some responsibility for increasing federal funding for that research by engaging the interest of other taxpayers, and by advocating it to our legislators.

References Cited

Meltzer, D.J.
1994 The Discovery of Deep Time: A History of Views on the
    Peopling of the Americas. In *Method and Theory for Investigating
    the Peopling of the Americas*, edited by R. Bonnichsen and D.G.
    Steele. Center for the Study of the First Americans, Oregon State
    University, Corvallis.

National Endowment for the Humanities
1994 *Composite List of Awards, 1966-1991, 1992, 1993, 1994.*
    Interpretive Research. National Endowment for the Humanities,
    Washington.

National Science Foundation (NSF)
1987 *Grant Lists, Fiscal Years 1978 to 1987.* National Science
    Foundation, Washington.

1993 Arctic Science, Engineering, and Education. Directory of
    Awards, Fiscal Year—1993. National Science Foundation,
    Arlington, Virginia.

1994 *Grant Lists, Fiscal Years 1990, 1991, and 1994.* National Science
    Foundation, Arlington, Virginia.

Seeking Private Funding for American Origins

Stephen Williams

The success of raising funds from private sector sources depends on a carefully considered approach. Key elements of the process consist of preparing a well structured request, personal contacts, knowing the interests and limitations of potential sources, and stewardship of grant sources. Hints for the successful quest for private funding and cautionary tales are provided from personal experiences.

The search for the origins of human settlement of the New World is surely not an inconsequential topic. It has great age, deep mystery, and some very exciting answers. And we, as New World archaeologists, have a public trust to see that this exciting enterprise is carried out diligently and with the best effort that time, money, and rational planning can provide. Public excitement certainly is a very big plus for the Paleoindian research projects that need to be carried out in the next decade. Of course there is more to raising money than just having an appealing topic, although that is a good start.

I will discuss the topic of seeking private funding for First Americans research the in four parts: (1) a well-structured request; (2) the need for personal contact; (3) known limits; and (4) stewardship.

The Request for Financial Support

We start with the *well-structured request*. This is in many ways not unlike a basic academic grant proposal, but honed down and dejargonized. It should contain a detailed budget and some interesting highlights of both the research and the hoped-for results. A well-wrapped product sells. You can't normally walk into a private foundation or a potential donor's office and ask for $10,000 for Paleoindian research and expect to walk out with the funds. If you can, then you're already at step two.

Moreover, even if you do know the donor that well, it will be more comfortable for both of you if you have in hand a programmatic document, however short, and a fairly detailed budget. The I.R.S. (U.S. Internal Revenue Service) likes it better that way too.

Personal Contacts

The second step is to *know your source personally*. Of course this is quite obvious if you are approaching an individual donor. However, it is just as true when you are dealing with a private foundation or a nonfederal granting agency; one way or another you've got to have a "hook."

I'm sure some of you could repeat verbatim the story of my own failure to get any help at all from some fifty private foundations that I importuned nearly twenty years ago. I researched the foundations very carefully, sent out heavy and well-documented project statements, spelling out chapter and verse of Ian Graham's exciting Maya hieroglyphic inscription project, and got *zero* response. Many never even acknowledged receipt of my request. We already had some very good support from several foundations for this project, which gave us the hope that others would be similarly interested. But the difference, of course, was that where we had been successful we had known someone, at least in the front office, if not the major donor. Our sample of fifty *new* foundations was derived from several foundation directories; we knew no one at any of them or, if we did, we didn't know how to tap them. So you will be wasting your time shooting blind, even if you are quite well informed as to the foundation's program; the package may never be looked at seriously unless you can write a truly personal covering letter or, better yet, precede it with a friendly phone call.

Now this can seem like a rather daunting task: how to find that hook. However, if your own institution has an advisory board of one sort or other, you should be able to query the members for possible foundation contacts. "Networking" they call it today—the Old Boy network of not so long ago. It is essential. It also means going to annual meetings and conferences, and showing the flag, and then sitting in smoke-filled rooms too late at night, finding out who knows who, and where special sources exist.

Personal contact is the essential ingredient. Sitting in a donor's office, or even better in his or her home, you can achieve a level of understanding and communication that you would absolutely never attain any other way, even with a fax machine.

I well remember a hot Fourth of July Bar-B-Que on Avery Island, Louisiana, just outside one of the old Tabasco warehouses, where Walter MacIlhenny got me backed into a corner and told me in no uncertain terms that it was high time to do some archaeology on the island. Now we had done *no* archaeology on the island at all, but I said, "Yes, sir, Mr. Walter, that certainly does sound reasonable." After all he was an ex-Marine Corps general and a real Hemingwayesque character. I'll also have to admit that it wasn't my project statement that got me started on a three-year, $75,000 program on Avery Island, but they all aren't like that.

Now private fund raising is not something taught at any graduate school. I have two more precepts to follow after (1) the simple request statement and (2) knowing someone personally who handles the purse strings, either their own or the foundation's.

What Can the Source Afford?

The third precept has a strong judgmental aspect and again is important in all fund raising requests: *know how much to ask for*. Look over previous lists of grants, or make a ballpark but thoughtful estimate of what sort of requests seems feasible from this particular donor. If you don't, you run the risk of getting the standard refusal: "We are truly interested in your project, but we have already allotted all the available funds for this year."

Few, especially private, donors will ever tell you directly that they can't *afford* such a large gift. Don't be fooled by appearances or even generous southern hospitality, for example. Know whether to ask for $500, $5,000, or $50,000. It is a crime to ask for too much and get turned down, but it's just as bad to ask for $500, and get it quickly, when you could have got $5,000. Foundations as well as individuals have in-house guidelines that you must scope out, and stick with. If you underestimate and get the grant, remember to check them out more carefully before you ask again; for you will be asking again, won't you?

Stewardship of Sources

That brings me to my final piece of obvious wisdom on fund raising: say *"thank you."* Do more than just send off the required letter of acknowledgment as you bank the check. Later, write the donor to let them know how the project is going and send them reports ("deliverables" in bureaucratese). Give them well-constructed letters of thanks—that's just as important as your starting request. And do keep in touch with them on a regular basis—we call this treatment of donors *stewardship*.

Remember, you will be asking again—maybe not this year, or even five years down the road. Therefore don't let the only letter they get from you, a year or two later, be a "please send more cash" document; that strategy may have worked with the folks back home when you were in college, but now you have to cultivate this field continually and carefully—here I am thinking primarily of private donors, but foundation personnel like to be treated as sentient beings too. Give them a slide show, a special tour of the lab, or a nicely done replica of a major find, a gift in return for a gift.

Although you may think of your contact with the donor as either intellectual ("they are impressed with the quality of my work"), or based on your obvious personal charisma, it is, in fact, a mixture of both. And don't ask too often. As the old Maine mink farmer responded when a visitor queried him about how often he took the pelts of the cunning little beasts:

"Well," he drawled, "they do get mighty nervous if you skin 'em more than once a year." He's right, and nervous donors are never any fun.

But cautionary tales abound, and some of them are even true. There *really* are little old ladies and men in tennis shoes out there, and they *are* looking for people and topics to support. Indeed, you may even find, to your obvious relief, that they really *enjoy* giving; all you need to do is give them the chance. But don't think you can turn that trick right away on first contact; patience is a virtue here too. They must get to know and trust you and your program before they'll write a check.

The fact is that lots of donors are deeply interested in the history of the American Indians; you can make that interest work for you. Look at your list of local amateurs. Really get to know some of them well; if they can't help you out with a check, maybe they know someone else who can. Also look for some really local foundations that have a special interest in the area. Finally, try what seems to be that toughest nut to crack, the corporate gift. Here's where a hook is downright essential. Many large business organizations have foundations or special officers responsible for giving. Get to know them—don't be shy, you're surely not the first nor the last to attempt to importune them and you've got nothing to lose by confessing your project over-run and consequent funding need.

Conclusions

One final piece of advice that I know you'll need. Don't get discouraged; no one bats a thousand. So be content with a modest .300 average. After all Wade Boggs doesn't do much better than that, on the playing field that is. Seriously, private fund raising is a nonstop enterprise at every institution. You come to the end of the fiscal year, proud of what you raised, and discouraged over the ones that got away; then the very next day you're off and running again. Will it never end? I know the answer but you don't want to hear it.

So take heart and remember that the most important step is to get that first gift from a donor or a foundation, even if it isn't at the level you might have hoped for. Once they've written that *first check* its up to you to prove to them that they've picked a winner.

Now I can't stress too much that giving is a very personal act—the funds may support your project, but they are truly given *to you*. Therefore *you're* on the firing line. Don't ever betray your donor's trust. Don't promise more than you can deliver. Hoopla and glitz may sell snake oil, secondhand cars, or even brand new Isuzus, but remember you'll be back next year, skinning knife in hand. Good luck.

U.S. Federal Funding: Resource and Land Management Support

John G. Douglas

Archaeological survey, excavation, and protection projects, costing many millions of dollars, are conducted each year on the vast federal land reserves of the United States, arguably with imperfect research focus. To help improve this focus and to turn these activities toward particular research ends, nonfederal archaeologists must become familiar with and actively involved in federal agency planning.

Before I come to the topic of U.S. federal agency funding for land and resource management and implications for research support, I want to talk generally about the administrative and geographical distribution of U.S. federal lands and the nature of managing agencies' missions, the ultimate point being to put the topic into what I hope might be a useful perspective for those who wish to influence research support. My remarks, while they unavoidably reflect the viewpoint I enjoy from the agency I work for (Bureau of Land Management [BLM]), represent only my personal views.

First, there are really very few federal land-managing agencies. Nearly seventy units of the government administer *some* land, ranging from the one-tenth of an acre charged to the federal Grain Inspection Service to the more than 270 million acres of the BLM. We can disregard most of the low end of the range. One million acres (404,700 hectares) makes a convenient dividing line to separate large from small land-holding agencies. This generally corresponds with agencies' self-identification as land managers, and it doesn't arbitrarily exclude any that just misses the cutoff (the nearest runner-up has many fewer acres). To help you visualize, 1 million acres would be contained by a square just under 40 miles (63.6 kilometers) on a side.

Almost one-third of the land surface of the United States, more than seven-tenths of a billion acres, is federally owned

(Bureau of Land Management 1989: Table 4). Only four cabinet departments and one government-owned corporation have responsibility for as much as one million acres. The Tennessee Valley Authority (TVA), the corporation, is just above the million-acre cutoff. Then there are the Department of Energy (DOE) with about 2.2 million acres, the Department of Defense (DoD) with about 25 million acres, the Department of Agriculture (USDA) with around 190 million acres, and the Department of the Interior (USDI) with more than 500 million acres. If you separate out from these three departments the subdivisions that themselves administer one million acres or more, the number of units that do so goes up to twelve. These dozen units are responsible for more than 99 percent of all federally owned land. Five are bureaus in USDI (BLM, Fish and Wildlife Service, National Park Service (NPS), Bureau of Indian Affairs, and Bureau of Reclamation) and four are subdivisions of DoD (Department of the Army, Department of the Air Force, Department of the Navy, and Army Corps of Engineers). The remaining three are the USDA's U.S. Forest Service (USFS), DOE Operations, and the TVA. After these twelve, more than fifty additional units account for the rest of the federal lands, a fraction of one percent, spread unevenly among them.

These few agencies that manage most of the federal lands and resources have most of their holdings in the western United States, including Alaska; the TVA is the single exception. About five-sixths of the lands held by the USFS are in western states, and virtually all of those held by the BLM are. So, too, are most of the units of the National Wildlife Refuge and National Park systems, and most of the DoD lands (General Services Administration 1989). Federal land and resource management issues, then, more often than not, are western issues within U.S. sociopolitics.

Within nonfederal circles in the western United States, close attention is paid to how federal management is done, what federal policies and precedents are established, and how the use of federal lands and resources is constrained. This reflects the fact that Alaska is 87 percent federally owned, Nevada 85 percent, Utah and Idaho each 63 percent, Wyoming 50 percent, Oregon 49 percent, California 46 percent, and so on. In contrast, all of the United States cut by or falling east of the 100th meridian, except for Florida and New Hampshire, count federal land percentages in single digits (Bureau of Land Management 1989: Table 4). A very substantial portion of the economy of the western United States depends on federal land and resource management.

The point of this recitation is to emphasize that nearly any discussion about managing federal lands and resources, including natural and cultural resources important to understanding the peopling of the Americas, will involve just a handful of agencies that tend to have a western frame of reference. They tend also to be newcomers at dealing with archaeology.

Management

Most federal agencies have become familiar with archaeological matters only since the early 1970s, in response to Title 36 *Code of Federal Regulations* (CFR) Part 800, the regulations that implement Section 106 of the National Historic Preservation Act (NHPA; Title 16 *U.S. Code* [U.S.C.] Section 470). Whether land managers or not, agencies whose actions or authorizations for others to act might have an effect on significant archaeological or historical properties must go through a closely defined accountability process before making a final decision to proceed (see Fowler, this volume). When the consulting participants determine that a proposed action would have an adverse effect on a significant property, the "Section 106 review process" usually concludes with an agreement ensuring that the adverse effects will be mitigated in an adequate manner, such as through partial data recovery in the case of an archaeological site that cannot be or need not be preserved in place. The proponent of the action, either the federal agency itself or the holder of a federal authorization, is then obligated to conduct the agreed-upon mitigation before proceeding with the action that prompted the review.

The Section 106 compliance process is, without question, the largest cause of federal and private expenditures for archaeology in the United States today (see Watson, Bonnichsen et al., this volume). Unfortunately, few people who are closely involved with it like it very much. Agency managers are often frustrated by it because it slows and adds unpredictability to the decision-making process; land use applicants who are required to pay consultants for surveys and mitigation projects are almost always annoyed by it because of the time and money that it requires; even archaeologists who carry it out are numbed by its routine nature. And archaeologists observing from outside, when they do, are likely to be disappointed with its orientation, outcome, or both. As the customary label of "compliance" would suggest, Section 106 review is something to be stoically lived through; and much of the time it is not very good science. It is certainly expensive in terms of finite archaeological resources as well as time and dollars, perhaps even in terms of good will toward archaeology and archaeologists. In parts of the West where there is substantial economic dependence on government lands and resources and where attitudes tend to favor minimal government regulation, archaeology is sometimes not a good topic for light discussion.

While Section 106 has created one kind of archaeological involvement in federal agencies, the Archaeological Resources Protection Act of 1979 as amended (ARPA; 16 U.S.C. 470 aa-mm) has created quite a different kind. In 1979, ARPA reinstated the ability of federal agencies to prosecute violators who dig in and/or remove artifacts from federal archaeological sites without a permit, an ability that had been hampered in much of the West by an earlier appeals court decision affecting the Antiquities Act of 1906. Like its precursor, ARPA is principally a criminal statute rather than one concerned with resource management. However, an amendment to ARPA now requires agencies to plan and schedule surveys to locate the scientifically most important archaeological resources—that is, those presumed to deserve the most careful protection from illegal disturbance or removal—thus adding a bit more management to the mix. The amendment is silent about authorizing funds for conducting such surveys as may be planned and scheduled. Incidentally, ARPA enforcement can be another source of strained public attitudes toward archaeology. In some western U.S. localities, hunting and digging for artifacts is viewed as a harmless traditional pastime, and arrests by government agents may stir deep local outrage.

The NHPA and ARPA, plus some related statutes of general scope and effect, can be seen to give a certain uniformity of purpose to land-managing agencies, applying in more or less the same ways to all. However, this veneer of uniformity may mask some major interagency differences. In addition to statutes with national application, most agencies follow their own agency-specific legislation, laws that give them particular missions and distinguish them from similar agencies. Much more than the national statutes, these laws are key to understanding a particular agency's viewpoint and culture.

Until the last decade or so, few of these mission-defining laws explicitly included archaeological and historical matters—the NPS organic act of 1916 being a notable exception—but now these matters are being incorporated among agency responsibilities as new laws are written and old ones are updated. The messages in this are that the Congress is aware and sensitive, at least at a problem-recognition level, and that land-managing agencies are perforce becoming more so. It appears safe to say that archaeology is securing a permanent place on the public agenda for federal lands. It is probably just as safe to say that most land-managing agencies are not yet completely comfortable with their new responsibilities.

Multiple Use Management

The two largest land-managing agencies, the BLM and USFS, are similar in mission as well as in immense size. These are the agencies whose specific legislation tells them to manage a full range of renewable and nonrenewable resources—all the things that are generally recognized as being resources—on the basis of multiple use and sustained yield. Sustained yield, when considered in terms of renewable resources such as timber and livestock forage, is fairly self explanatory. The concept of multiple use hinges on balance and informed choice, the combination of land and resource uses that will best accommodate both present demand and future needs. It is a conservation concept intended to promote forward-looking and thoughtful use of the nation's assets owned in common.

Two federal acres out of three are managed by the BLM or USFS. Two federal acres out of three are managed for multiple use. Part of the importance of this lies in the fact that these two agencies are painstaking planners—in order to find that proper combination of land and resource uses—and planning is very much open to public participation, needs it, depends on it. The further implication is that archaeologists have a genuine opportunity to make their special knowledge and research interests part of the basis on which particular federal lands are managed, an opportunity that is almost always overlooked.

Research Funding

Now, after all that preamble, there is not much to say about archaeological or archeologically related research funding by land-managing agencies. In these years of continuing budget deficits and relative austerity in domestic programs, it is gratifying, I suppose, that the small amount of federal spending for cultural resources—archaeology and history—seems to stay fairly constant, keeping pace with inflation. The President's budget submissions to the Congress may call for decreases, but the Congress usually restores the prior year's level with a little extra, to help keep up with increased costs of doing business and to respond in modest ways to new, congressionally directed emphases. For example, the Congress has emphasized ARPA protection in the late 1980s and early 1990s, particularly with regard to agencies' law enforcement capabilities.

I can't tell you exactly how much money is involved. Just as federal agencies operate under their own agency-specific laws, fulfilling their individual missions, they have evolved their own ways of categorizing, requesting, and accounting for appropriated funds. Different agencies count money differently. Consequently, it is difficult or impossible to compare budget figures across agency lines and have reasonable assurance that like items are being compared.

More useful than raw appropriation or budget figures are the numbers agencies compile and submit for the Secretary of the Interior's annual report to the Congress on federal archaeological activities (Knudson and McManamon 1992; see also Keel et al. 1989, McManamon et al. 1993). For the 43 agencies responding to the questionnaires for fiscal years 1985 and 1986, it appears that about $75-$80 million (in appropriated funds) is being spent each year, roughly 95 percent going to NHPA compliance and most of the remainder to ARPA enforcement. There is no way to determine how much private money goes to NHPA compliance.

Can any of this funding be made available to support academically significant archaeological research in the nonfederal sector (see Bonnichsen and others, this volume)? Perhaps, if the research questions were defined in terms of an agency's management needs, and communicated to the agency in usable ways. Few land-managing agencies would identify basic research as an agency priority. While they will almost always try to bring research relevance to bear on decisions affecting archaeological resources, agencies generally have to scramble to accomplish the things they are legally required to do; this tends to give them a narrow, pragmatic, somewhat stingy outlook. Even if a required task consists mainly of gathering and understanding new archaeological data, it may not be spoken of as "research"; in federal land-managing agency jargon, "research" may well carry connotations of frivolity or ivory-tower impracticality. If one looks closely, though, many practical, mission-oriented operations really are research, lacking little in preparation, execution, analysis, or interpretation but phrased in practical, bureaucratic terms. And due to a tight focus, a management study conducted under contract—research of a task-adapted, applied sort—may inadvertently neglect to explore some of a topic's or a study area's research potential. It bears mention that academically based researchers seldom compete for contracts to do management studies.

Planning

I spoke briefly of planning. For the sake of discussion, federal
land management planning can be seen as being of two kinds.
The first is a more leisurely kind, conducted over many months,
that examines quantitative, qualitative, and spatial data for a
comprehensive range of natural and cultural resources, supply and demand issues, potential conflicts, competing public
interests, and numerous other factors. This kind of planning
produces relatively complete, long-term, resource allocation
and land use prescriptions, a basis for future management. The
second is a much more immediate kind of compliance-driven
planning that involves a relatively more hurried review of iden-
tifiable environmental conflicts, a weighing of apparent
consequences, a comparison of options, some selected public
participation, and a decision. As should be intuitively evident,
planning of the latter kind is more likely to yield good decisions if planning of the former kind has already been done
and done thoroughly.

As I previously noted, the archaeological profession is
largely uninvolved in planning by federal land-managing agencies, whether long-term management planning or short-term,
compliance-driven planning (see Bonnichsen et al., this volume). This is surely one of the main reasons why federal
cultural resource management is subject to criticism as so-so
science. Few archaeologists seem to have realized that federal
agencies are accountable to the public for their policies, procedures, plans, and performance, and that they are truly open to
helpful information, ideas, and suggestions.

Allow me to quote several paragraphs from another paper
I presented in early 1989:

> If you were to ask a good sample of people who deal
> regularly with cultural resources what cultural re-
> source management means, they'd surely almost all
> say something about Section 106 compliance. Many
> would equate the two, considering them to be exact
> synonyms. Don't get me wrong, Section 106 is a good
> tool for historic preservation, a proven means for

making federal agencies accountable, and I and many like me owe our jobs to it. But Section 106 compliance is not *cultural resource* management, it's *undertaking* management, *project* management, administrative *process* management.

We typically go into it with too little time and a dearth of knowledge, discover things we scarcely anticipated, apply a woefully inadequate set of screening criteria, make some half-informed mitigation decisions, collect the standard data, and never look back. We can't look back, we're too busy doing it all over again somewhere else. With repetition we get pretty good at it, but our proficiency is geared to applying the process, not to managing the resources. Maybe it's not quite that bleak and mindless; we actually do save some things that should be saved (and maybe some we needn't bother over), and we improve our feel for what's important as we go along. But we're not *managing* cultural resources.

I can't imagine a construction under which historic preservation including reactive Section 106 compliance (and archaeological resource protection including reactive law enforcement, for that matter) would not be *part* of cultural resource management. But there has to be more to management than reaction. . . .

If the archaeological profession collectively wants . . . good management for archaeological resources, then individual archaeologists must be active in sharing what they know, and think, and can figure out. . . .

[F]ind out which [federal agency] office administers the lands and the archaeology you're interested in, ask where they are in the planning cycle, get on their mailing list, do some research, and participate. Think of it as *pro bono* work—we should be at least as noble as lawyers (Douglas 1989).

Participation

Many concerned individuals, industry representatives, special interest groups, and others with an economic or policy stake in the management of federal lands and resources actively involve themselves in the work of government, visiting field offices, talking with staff and managers, attending public meetings, reading and commenting on draft decision documents, offering helpful suggestions, influencing the outcome. For archaeologists to neglect to do this is to entrust the care of archaeological resources, including the research uses—if any—to which they are put, blindly to others. Overextended and pressured agency staff will do the best job they can. However, if they don't happen to know the things you know, or to value the things you value, you can be reasonably sure that your interests will not be weighed in agency decisions. Please do not let that happen.

References Cited

Bureau of Land Management
1989 *Public Land Statistics* Vol. 173 (1988). U.S. Department of the
    Interior, Washington.

Douglas, J.G.
1989 Why Not Manage Cultural Resources? In "Cultural Resource
    Management in the 1990s," edited by P.S. Miller, D.E. Gelburd,
    and G.A. Alderton, pp. 63-70. *American Society for Conservation
    Archaeology Proceedings 1989.*

Keel, B.C., F.P. McManamon, and G.S. Smith (compilers)
1989 *Federal Archeology: The Current Program. Annual Report to
    Congress on the Federal Archeological Program FY 1985 and FY 1986.*
    U.S. Department of the Interior, National Park Service,
    Washington.

Knudson, R., and F.P. McManamon
1992 The Secretary's Report to Congress on the Federal Archeology
    Program. *Federal Archeology Report* 5(2):1,4-9.

McManamon, F.P., P.S. Knoll, R. Knudson, G.S. Smith, and R.C.
Waldbauer (compilers)
1993 *Federal Archeological Programs and Activities.* U.S. Department
    of the Interior, National Park Service, Archeological Assistance
    Division, Departmental Consulting Archeologist, Washington.

VII. Summary

The conference reported in part in this volume was organized as an international scientific research exposition, with the Public Trust Symposium added as an afterthought. Because of the present differences between the cultures—including language, structure, function, and values—of public archaeologists and academy researchers, communication between the two worlds is difficult. Few people cross over effectively between the two domains. Even at the May 1989 Summit Conference, there did not appear to be much communication—"researchers" were very involved in the first three days of "scientific" papers, and most left before the Public Trust Symposium. Many of the symposium participants, most of whom are "cultural resource managers," did not attend all of the first three days' presentations and came to the conference almost exclusively to participate in the symposium.

Yet, probably all conference participants, if asked, would say that they believe that First Americans resources are of significant public scientific and humanistic value, and that their conservation is a major public policy issue.

The post-conference interaction among scientific, educational, and managerial interests has been significant, and this volume with its explicit linkages of these various elements is an exciting project to have generated and seen to fruition.

The final paper by Keel and Calabrese reviews the public context in which First Americans archaeological and paleo-environmental resources will be conserved, used, or consumed—a public management context. Together with the other papers in this volume they provide guidance for the future of the distant past.

Ruthann Knudson

Stewardship of First Americans Resources

Bennie C. Keel & F.A. Calabrese

The Public Trust Doctrine is an appropriate concept under which to develop First Americans stewardship policies and programs, and is embedded in the U.S. authorizing legislation establishing agencies such as the Smithsonian Institution, National Park Service, and Bureau of Land Management. First Americans research sponsored by national land-managing agencies should have two goals: to collect new information for use in public understanding of the past, and to assist the agencies in managing the archeological sites, materials, and information for which they are responsible. Both avocational and professional archaeologists need to become more involved in the development and implementation of environmental legislation, ensuring that it includes protection of archaeological or other materials critical to understanding the First Americans, so that these resources are managed as part of broader air, water, and land management. Public awareness of First Americans archeological protection needs is a critical factor in implementing a public trust concept.

The Public Trust

It is appropriate that this volume should begin with the concept of the public trust (Knudson, Le Master) in archaeology. It is through this concept that in the United States today we have the philosophy, ethic, laws, and management (stewardship) principles which allow us to protect our archaeological resources—be they the remains of the First Americans or a historical military or civilian encampment representing the western expansion in the territories held by the descendants of those First Americans—as well as natural resources.

The concept of a public trust is stated rather simply and without equivocation in the 1916 act establishing the National

---

If no publication dates are noted with a bibliographic citation in this chapter, the referenced document is included within this volume and is not included in the cited references for this chapter.

Park Service (NPS) as an agency responsible ". . . to conserve the scenery and the natural and historic objects and the wildlife therein and to provide for the enjoyment of the same in such a manner and by such means as will leave them unimpaired for the enjoyment of future generations" (*Public Law* [P.L.] 235, 39 *Statutes-at-Large* [Stat.] 535, 16 *U.S. Code* [U.S.C.] 1 et seq.). Implicit in this statement is not only the construct of preservation as the objective of policy and law, but the facts of how we are to treat the resource (it is to be left "unimpaired") and why we preserve it ("for the enjoyment of future generations"). These words impose the full force of a public trust upon the NPS.

The 1916 act embodies concepts which developed in the late 1880s about the preservation of lands for future generations, reflecting the philosophies of President Theodore Roosevelt (in office 1901-1909) and naturalist John Muir (1838-1914). While the concept was first embodied in the establishment of our national parks and significant historic resources (Hot Springs, Arkansas, in the 1860s and Yellowstone 1872) it is not unique to the United States. In fact, while the United States was initially setting aside lands as preserves, the Canadian government was the first to establish a central managing agency, Parks Canada, in 1895.

The concept of a public trust in preservation has its roots in the preservation of natural areas, to which were added historical and, by extension, archaeological, resources. The same preservation ethic resulted in the United States in the establishment of the Smithsonian Institution (1849), as well as the Bureau of American Ethnology (1879), entities with a mission to preserve the knowledge of indigenous peoples and lifeways before their total eradication and loss. And, while the philosophy of an ethic of public trust is manifest in the protection of large land areas, the legal backbone for much of the acquisition of such preserves in the United States rests upon the Antiquities Act of 1906, legislation designed to protect archaeological and historically significant remains (P.L. 59-209, Stat. 335, 16 U.S.C. 431-433).

The concept of public trust is also embedded in legislation of other major federal land-managing agencies in the United

States (Douglas), with the Federal Land Policy and Management Act of 1976 (P.L. 94-579) giving similar responsibilities to the Bureau of Land Management. Although within the U.S. Department of the Interior (USDI) the various land-managing agencies may have different management directives, e.g., multiple use and conservation vs. preservation, the public trust ethic is explicit and should pervade the management decision-making process. It does not always happen in the ideal fashion for the reasons addressed by Le Master.

The problems resulting from pressures upon First Americans resources from competing private, and sometimes public, interests (Le Master) are most readily observed in explicit acts to obtain natural resources held in protected land preserves, e.g., oil in Alaska and the coastal areas, coal in the Dakotas, wetlands development in suburban areas. The taking of these resources by private companies seemingly impacts only the natural environment, but these actions almost always involve extensive land modification, with the resulting potential loss of subsurface archaeological resources. While archaeological resources appear to be protected in conjunction with our lands in "public trust," protection is often compromised by outright shifts in federal administration policy concerning drilling, mining, or land use, or purposeful neglect through funding shifts (Le Master). Areas assumed to be best preserved, such as national parks, can be compromised by shifts in management philosophies at not only the national but the regional and even the local level. In short, while there is sufficient legislation to protect and preserve, that ethic is easily undermined both consciously and unconsciously in a number of ways.

The application of a public trust philosophy and ethic to private land holdings seems an insurmountable problem in the United States, given our fierce belief in private ownership of property. But there are breaks developing in that armor, as noted by Fowler. Historical and prehistoric burial remains and associated grave goods on private lands are being protected, irrespective of their antiquity. And consensual arrangements are being made for protection and preservation (e.g., privately held sites on the National Register of Historic Places).

A shift in U.S. philosophy concerning the protection of antiquities to one similar to those in Asian and/or South American countries is not out of the question—even though a long shot. But as Le Master notes, in a representative democracy, the public (and archaeologists) have an opportunity to direct that philosophy and ethic. It is up to us to shape them or at least to nudge them in a specific direction. The legislation that is in place to protect and preserve resources on U.S. public lands came about through evolutionary rather than revolutionary changes in mandates; as that evolution continues, there may also be a shift in the concepts that are adapted to the protection, preservation, and management (stewardship) of the archaeological resources.

The sum total of U.S. public policy for archaeology can be viewed, as Le Master considers it, as " . . . a mosaic of policy statements contained in the laws, administrative rules, court decisions, recent presidential budget requests, and congressional appropriations acts . . . " (and the situation is probably similar in most other countries). That is how our collective attitude about the public trust is made manifest. If that is the case, then we are indeed in trouble, for we archaeologists collectively have not worked well in our own best interests.

As some must require a leap of faith to assert that archaeological resources are part of a public trust, public archaeologists can only ask academic scholarly archaeologists to extend that "leap of faith" to some of their colleagues—to those who have ventured into the world of resource management within the federal as well as state government, to those who have worked hard to see the concept of public trust become the overriding management philosophy, while yet retaining the ability to integrate research into the management doctrine.

For some within the U.S. federal, tribal, and state cultural resource management (CRM) systems, it has been frustrating to witness the direction that archaeologists and archaeological programs have taken in general preservation programs. A statement that Calabrese made to a former professor in 1974 came to be true: "Train your students well, and remember those who do not go on to become researchers may and will seek employment in the state and local governments; and they will dictate the future archaeology will take in this country." Calabrese did not realize at that time the full impact of what he was predicting. Now archaeological protection compliance procedures are required of federal agencies and private companies, performed by staff archaeologists trained by the academic researchers, and most frequently under the guidance of State Historic Preservation Office (SHPO) staffs. Thus, too many archaeological programs must be carried out by key staff members who are, as Douglas comments, "numbed by the routine of it," pursuing tasks that must be "stoically lived through" to facilitate archeological work that ends up as "not good science." Whose fault is that? It is ours, not anyone else's.

To be sure, as Bonnichsen et al. point out, federal archaeological programs in the United States have taken a turn we did not expect and there has been an interest in building administrative structures to control archaeology. Perhaps the result of any legislation is the development of a bureaucracy to implement it. But that does not mean that the interests of science and research cannot be served. If those laws, rules, decisions, policy statements, and budget requests reflect our collective public policy and serve as underpinnings for our public trust ethic and in a representative democracy, as Le Master notes, we control that policy, then we must collectively take full responsibility for our actions concerning the public trust. Archaeologists cannot hide in ivory towers (basement anthropology labs) or government citadels (small windowless offices) and place responsibility for our current state of affairs on anyone else.

Calabrese (1976) pointed out that, about the time the Moss-Bennett bill passed the U.S. Congress in 1974, archaeologists created an environment that encouraged the rise of contract archaeology (cf. Bonnichsen et al.). At that time there was an opportunity to develop an institutional framework to guide the management of archaeological programs with a research-oriented philosophy. But there were few advocates of such a policy, and even fewer scholars were aware that, while the legislation might protect resources, it would not provide better scholarship and research. Those responsible for overseeing federal archaeological programs at that time were not promoting a research approach, but rather alternative policies which led to our current federal management programs.

Research

It is clear from the papers in this volume that philosophies on the direction archaeology should take differ between researchers within and outside of federal or state agencies. On the one hand, Bonnichsen et al. lament programs stressing survey and inventory for "place oriented" federal agencies and archaeological programs to promote avoidance, while on the other hand Calabrese has recently told the NPS Associate Director for Cultural Resources that the biggest contribution the NPS can make is to "inventory . . . inventory . . . inventory." Without doubt the needs of the land-managing agencies and researchers do not always coincide, but these disparate approaches need to be mutually understood and valued. They do not necessarily prohibit and can support desirable research in First Americans studies.

Those who promote CRM as the ultimate objective of public trust archaeology often control the dollars that are used and needed to accomplish archaeological projects and programs. Some people have worked hard to integrate the concepts of conservation and preservation (Lipe and Lindsey 1974) with research in federal archaeological programs; however, not all federal archeology programs are tied to compliance- or development-related archaeology. There are a large number of programs in the United States integrating public and academic archaeology within the federal system, in both compliance-related programs and programs designed for long-term development of information for scholarly and public consumption. A number of such information-development programs have been carried out by researchers within the NPS Midwest Archeological Center, and through cooperative agreements with major universities. The examples below are only a sampling.

The Knife River Archaeological Program in North Dakota began as a cooperative program between the NPS and the University of North Dakota, designed to provide data for a newly established park area. A research design was developed which brought together researchers in geomorphology, geography, anthropology, ethnohistory, physics, mathematics, and computer science to evaluate archaeological remains at the Knife River Indian Villages National Historic Site area from the Paleoindian to the present. While the emphasis was upon the last one thousand years, funds were also expended to work outside the park area to evaluate the local geomorphology and test a number of sites in conjunction with privately funded research in the area. This resulted in the location of one of the earliest Paleoindian sites in North Dakota as well as a number of Archaic archaeological sites. The results of this project included more than thirty monographs, several masters theses and two dissertations, a four-volume summary series of scientific information, a book designed as a synthesis for the layman and for public education (Ahler et al. 1991), and a second book for children (Ward et al. 1989).

Another project conducted as rescue archaeology evolved in the Grand Teton National Park in Wyoming, as the Bureau of Reclamation (BoR) drew down the waters of the artificially raised Jackson Lake in preparation for the rebuilding of the Jackson Lake Dam. With the water levels lowered, a number of important archaeological sites were exposed. A survey of the area was initiated to locate other sites that might have been inundated since the 1906 construction of the original dam. Over one hundred previously drowned sites were recorded. As part of the project, a research design was developed to guide the survey and succeeding mitigation program. Part of this design was a systematic program, employing the work of Pleistocene-Holocene research geologist Ken Pierce, to discover paleosoils where Paleoindian sites might be located and evaluated. There were funding constraints and time constraints, but then when are there not in government programs? Given all of the limitations, a sincere effort was made to locate and evaluate (excavate) Paleoindian sites as well as representative samples of all other sites. Unfortunately, for a variety of reasons, although surface manifestations suggested the presence of Paleoindian remains, they were not found in the subsurface formations, though they are well represented in surface collections made around the lake for decades.

Harney Flats in Florida (Daniel and Wisenbaker 1987) was a large (3.36 acres, 1.35 hectare) Late Paleoindian-Early Archaic site. The archaeological recovery project conducted there was funded by the U.S. Department of Transportation and the Florida Department of Transportation, and was carried out by the Florida Bureau of Archaeological Research. Some 967m² of the earliest components were excavated. Through careful excavations and piece plotting, the investigators were able to construct distributions which led to the identification of activity areas and understanding of the site function and plan. The final report provides an excellent record of the material and data recovered that can be used to further the understanding of First Americans complexes.

Explicit efforts were made in the development of the U.S. Army Corps of Engineers (COE) Richard B. Russell Reservoir in Georgia and South Carolina to identify and examine Paleoindian sites within the project area, within the overall preconstruction cultural resource inventory and evaluation effort. This effort was planned as a joint research program by the COE, NPS, Georgia and South Carolina state archaeologists, SHPO staffs, and elements of the professional community. Some eight to ten professional archaeologists were involved in developing the research parameters for this project. A synthesis as well as a critical critique of the Russell research program are presented in Anderson and Joseph (1988). The results of First Americans research there were quite informative, although no major *in situ* Paleoindian components were found and investigated. Nonetheless, small buried Paleoindian components were excavated at several sites and the methods used and reports of these efforts provide exceptionally good data.

At the same time, a few miles southeast of the Russell Reservoir area, Paleoindian research was being conducted by the University of Georgia in the Wallace Reservoir on the Oconee River. This was part of a program to mitigate the effects of the proposed Wallace Reservoir construction, and was supported by the Georgia Power Company. The Wallace Reservoir investigations have been published by the University of Georgia (Brook 1991, Fish and Hally 1983, Ledbetter et al. 1981, O'Steen et al. 1986). Information acquired from these as well as other Paleoindian investigations in Georgia and the surrounding states has been synthesized in Anderson et al. (1990).

Additional CRM projects in the United States in which First Americans research concerns were imbedded in the implementing stages of mitigation efforts or grew out of initial CRM investigations are listed below, with their sponsoring agencies and resulting publications:

- Tennessee-Tombigbee, Alabama and Tennessee (COE and NPS; Brose 1991)
- Southwest Jefferson County, Kentucky Flood Control Project (COE and NPS; Collins 1979)
- I-270 Project, Illinois (Illinois Department of Transportation, NPS, and Illinois Archaeological Survey; Bareis and Porter 1984)
- New Melones Dam and Reservoir, California (COE, NPS, and BoR; Moratto et al. 1988)
- Central Arizona Project, Arizona (BoR)
- Dolores Project, Colorado (BoR; Breternitz et al. 1986)
- Daniel Boone National Forest, Kentucky (U.S. Forest Service; Bush and Thomas 1986a, 1986b, Ison 1988)
- Delaware Water Gap, Pennsylvania and New Jersey (COE and NPS; Orr and Campana 1991)
- Tellico Reservoir, Tennessee (NPS and Tennessee Valley Authority [TVA]; Chapman 1985)
- Normandy Reservoir Project, Tennessee (TVA; Faulkner and McCollough 1973)

The results of these investigations and the insights they have produced have not been relegated to the grey literature, but have been published in monographs distributed to the public without charge.

Federal and state archaeological programs in the United States are compatible with First Americans research objectives, if the principal representatives of the federal and state agencies involved have a research orientation. The divorce of research from CRM is not a reflection of legislation, but of the attitude of the archaeologists serving as advisors to the managers of the resource.

Public archaeology has produced a huge volume of monograph-size publications outlining the results of surveys, data recovery, and evaluation statements. These are often available only in manuscript form (the government certainly can not afford to publish them all) sent to interested scholars and distributed as grey literature (though see discussion of the National Archaeological Data Base in McManamon and Knudson, this volume). But to say that anyone wishing to do research with this literature must spend innumerable hours separating out valuable data from legally required documentation is an overstatement, and suggests that these researchers are becoming a bit lazy. Who said that research is easy or not time consuming? With some familiarity, these documents can be scanned and digested quite easily. If one is to contribute to the search for the First Americans, one must become familiar with the available data—all of it. Who ever promised that it would be neatly synthesized and pre-digested and regurgitated first?

In fact a number of benefits have derived from the CRM programs in U.S. federal, tribal, state, and local agencies.

Throughout the United States, in SHPOs and other government agency offices, are computerized listings of known archeological sites and cultural affiliations as well as electronic bibliographies of the available grey literature reporting these sites (McManamon and Knudson, this volume). One can predict that as we forge further into the computer age, additional data will become available to researchers in the office and at home without the need to travel to the area of interest. It is far better now than it was in the past. Archaeological information gathering in the late 1960s and through the 1980s in the United States required searching through unorganized site records in musty basements and personal libraries of professors for obscure papers and little-known and often unpublished data. The problem continues, the volume of data is greater, and federal agencies are attempting to use the best available methods for managing and controlling this information.

Legal Aspects

Several chapters in this volume (Fowler, Le Master, Magne, McGimsey) covering the legal environment provide a basic framework for understanding opportunities and constraints in conducting archaeological research in general. It is not surprising that some Central and South American countries have stronger legislation than the United States to protect the nation's interest in controlling sites, objects, and monuments of the civilizations represented in their history. Unlike sites containing evidence of earlier cultures, the remains of the high cultures are impressive, even to the common citizen, and there is genetic continuity between a large proportion of past and present peoples there.

Laws and their emphasis reflect the particular history of the individual national government. The coverage or protective depth that the laws reach reflect the political philosophies of current governments. Irrespective of the amount of coverage offered by these laws, a common basic underpinning is conservation of each nation's archaeological record for the benefit of its citizens. How those benefits are to accrue is not spelled out in the laws.

There seems to be a common view across much of the world that archaeological or historic preservation laws are some how anti-research because they do not stipulate "research" in their language. Some managers and decision makers in the United States make this interpretation, but most of them have been swayed from this position by crafty agency archaeologists who have been able to develop research-like programs though the thoughtful manipulation of compliance project planning and contracting language. Instances can be cited to show that researchers have used political connections to expand and augment CRM projects to parallel their research interests. Elsewhere in this chapter we have described research efforts related to First Americans studies which have been carried out within the existing body of preservation rules and regulations. In each case these efforts were developed through the close cooperation of "researchers" and government archaeologists.

We believe that most public agencies in North America welcome well-designed research projects within their domains. The normal requirements to conduct research on USDI lands, for example, are pretty simple: a practical explicit research design; competent researchers; the wherewithal to conduct the program, including funds, equipment, institutional backing, and a record of successful research; and a program that does not interfere with other agency missions, particularly the mission of the land unit where investigations are to take place. Frequently, flexibility in scheduling field work will overcome conflict with other mission objectives. Contrary to sentiments expressed by some of our colleagues, we see the purpose of conservation archaeology as not to lock out research, but rather to assure that resources are wisely consumed.

Archaeologists in countries that are just beginning to formulate or redefine environmental legislation need to become deeply involved in such efforts. Participation at the beginning of the legislative process may allow for the legal authorization of specific archaeological values up front, rather than the need to continually struggle to sneak such values under the tent at a later time.

Public Education and Awareness

We find ourselves singing in the same choir as do many other authors in this volume when it comes to the need for greater public education of the laity, politicians, Native Americans, and decision makers. Clearly there is great need for archaeology to gain as much public support as possible. The experiences reported by Devine and Bense show that several segments of the public are interested in playing a role in archaeology. The roles that they wish to play may be active ones ranging from field or laboratory volunteer activities to serving as site stewards or clients of archaeological entertainment. We encourage researchers to devise as many opportunities as possible for public participation. Our experience has been that members of the public are willing to put up with the same difficulties and frustrations as paid crew members in field work. They are frequently willing to go beyond the efforts of paid personnel in the laboratory.

In the United States over the last decade, a significant effort has been made by the USDI, Society for American Archaeology (SAA), several SHPOs, and other parties to halt vandalism and the destruction of archaeological resources. The attack on this problem has several facets. In 1985, the USDI's Departmental Consulting Archaeologist instituted the collection and dissemination of data concerning illegal archaeological activities and began reporting them to Congress (Knudson and McManamon 1992; see Keel et al. 1989, McManamon et al. 1993). Simultaneously, a data base for the collection and dissemination of information about archaeology education programs (Knoll 1990, 1993) was instituted. In 1988, ARPA was amended to reduce the felony threshold for offenses under the Act, make intent to violate the Act an offense, and require agencies to pursue inventory of archaeological resources on the public lands in a more systematic and timely manner.

Also in 1988, the SAA initiated a public archeological resource protection project with the help of federal funding. This initiative resulted in meetings of concerned professionals in Taos, New Mexico (SAA 1991), and in Las Vegas, Nevada (Smith and Ehrenhardt 1991), devoted to identifying problems and defining practical solutions. The results of these conferences are similar to the ideas expressed by Bonnichsen et al. in this volume.

At the national level, the USDI recognizes exemplary efforts of public and private sector groups to conserve the nation's resources through its Public Service Awards program. Recent recipients include Gulf Power Company (Florida) for its Hawkshaw Project (Bense 1985), George Gummerman, Southern Illinois University-Carbondale for the Black Mesa, Arizona project, and Fred Wendorf, Southern Methodist University, for his career-long efforts in public archaeology. Also at the national level, the President's Advisory Council on Historic Preservation operates an awards program in which archaeological preservation projects have been recognized (ACHP 1993:8). A number of states and state-level archaeological societies as well as the SAA (Crabtree Award) and Canadian Archaeological Association present annual recognition awards to deserving individuals or groups. The media attention given to the recipients of these awards furthers education of the general public regarding the desirability of the wise use of the nation's archaeological resources.

The NPS is currently conducting an Earliest Americans National Historic Landmark (NHL) Theme Study (Grumet et al. 1995) to recognize and protect significant First Americans sites. Designation of First Americans NHLs on public and private lands, and distribution of information about them, will support research and enhance awareness of Late Pleistocene-Holocene climates and environments, and human adaptation to and use of those environments.

Our impression is that over the last few years there has been an increase in the number of societies or foundations that promote archaeological research and conservation. There also seems to be a slight growth in the memberships of state-level avocational societies, which may be generated by the opportunity for more active participation at the local level. In at least one state, North Carolina, two statewide archaeological organizations—the Archaeological Society of North Carolina, whose operation has been guided by the University of North Carolina-Chapel Hill, and the Friends of North Carolina Archeology, operated out of the Department of Cultural Resources in Raleigh—have merged into a single strong organization. Both bodies believed that as a single voice they would have a stronger impact on the state house in matters related to the state's archaeological programs. We believe that these examples of increased public participation in archeological activities can be attributed to a greater level of awareness of the status of and threats to U.S. archaeological resources.

Funding

First Americans researchers need to become more aware of the multitude of potential sources for funding their studies.

We expect that scholars involved in active research are fully aware of the traditional funding bodies within their own nations. In the United States, academicians most commonly name the National Science Foundation (NSF) and the National Geographic Society (NGS) as archaeological research support agencies. Wealthy individuals or tax shelter foundations created by industry are other sources of support. Support from the general public through fund-raising activities has become more common in the United States in recent years; in England, archaeology through public subscription has been around for some time. The largest source of funding for First Americans research in the United States probably is to be found in state and federal agencies as they meet their cultural resource management responsibilities.

Williams has provided excellent guidance on the care and feeding of private funding sources. It should not be surprising that the recommendations he provides are also directly applicable to developing and maintaining a positive relationship with government agencies. Douglas gives a particularly clear picture of the intricacies of CRM planning and funding in a major U.S. land-managing agency. His discussion of the interaction between researchers and his agency parallels comments made by Williams. The key seems to be communication between agency managers and researchers. As Watson notes, funding for direct or related First Americans research in the recent past has comprised about six percent of the $2-$3 million awarded annually by NSF to archaeological activities. During the 1978-87 decade, NSF thus spent about $1.5 million on Paleoindian research. Referring back to Watson's partial list of federal CRM projects involving First Americans research, we suggest that substantially more was spent by the federal government through its historic preservation activities than through direct research funding.

Investigators pursuing funds for First Americans research in the United States should consider broadening their horizons. Given that the Congress has directed federal land-managing agencies to develop specific plans to identify the important federally owned archaeological resources, the time is ripe for First Americanists to participate in guiding this effort.

Recommendations

First Americans research is important in delineating the initial peopling of the Americas, but it is only a small part of each nation's overall public archaeological programs. Manifestations of later cultural complexes are more apparent and more easily located and recorded than those representing the first inhabitants. It is important to recognize this fact, so that in each major land-development project sufficient effort is made to employ a multidisciplinary research approach that will allow for evaluation of the potential for Paleoindian remains, and to take every opportunity to fill in that segment of the archaeological record. But the remainder of the record should not, of course, be slighted.

This approach is dependent upon First Americans scholars becoming familiar with and accustomed to working with archaeologists and land managers involved in overseeing public archaeological programs. It is also dependent upon public archaeologists insuring that those involved in First Americans research are notified about, and their talents and knowledge integrated into, research plans and programs where the potential exists for unraveling First Americans questions.

The public trust philosophy and ethic must be stressed and promoted at every opportunity. There has been a recent trend to foster that awareness through "archaeology weeks" (Greengrass 1993) and through communication of basic information to the public by public agencies. Additional emphasis is needed. In large public projects involving archaeology, sufficient funds must be programmed to develop books for a lay audience, including children, in several languages. Videos, brochures, booklets, and posters can convey to the public considerable information and develop an archaeological awareness not otherwise found. First Americans scholars must take the time to develop these media, to write in a format that is conceptually different from that in which they are trained. They must accept and even support the fact that funds they might believe better spent on research are being used to promote archaeological public education and awareness.

The concept of a public trust, already noted in U.S. land-managing policies, must be stressed for our cultural properties as well as natural resources. The philosophy and ethic is there, but the relationship to archaeological resources must be stated explicitly. Further development of the public trust concept as it relates to private property rights must await a shift in the collective public philosophy. To force or attempt to direct that shift may alienate the public more than it would persuade them of the notion that archeological resources are a public trust.

Funding of First Americans research, or any other archaeology for that matter, is not going to increase in the near future. Slight increases in funding may occur, but it is likely that archaeological funding levels will remain stagnant or decrease relative to spending in other segments of the economy. Funding for archaeology in the United States is in large part tied to funding of public trust land-managing agencies. That in turn is tied to administrative and congressional actions. The reality in most nations is that funding for archaeology is tied to economic prosperity, and will increase only when the collective national disposable income changes. Given other social program needs, archaeology does not stand much of a chance for budgetary increases. Archaeologists must seek private (foundation and individual) funding for our special First Americans projects, and insure that First Americans research is considered and included in existing and future public programs.

References Cited

Advisory Council on Historic Preservation (ACHP)
1993 *Report to the President and Congress of the United States 1993.*
   Advisory Council on Historic Preservation, Washington.

Ahler, S.A., T.D. Thiessen, and M.K. Trimble
1991 *People of the Willows: The Prehistory and Early History of the Hidatsa Indians.* University of North Dakota Press, Grand Forks.

Anderson, D.G., and J.W. Joseph
1988 *Prehistory and History Along the Upper Savannah River: Technical Synthesis of Cultural Resource Investigations, Richard B. Russell Multiple Resource Area*, Vols I and II. Russell Papers, Interagency Archeological Services Division. U.S. Department of the Interior, National Park Service, Atlanta, Georgia.

Anderson, D.G., R.J. Ledbetter, and L. O'Steen
1990 Paleoindian Period Archaeology of Georgia. *University of Georgia Laboratory of Archaeology Series Report* No. 28; *Georgia Archaeological Research Design Paper* No. 6.

Bareis, C.J., and J.W. Porter
1984 *American Bottom Archaeology.* University of Illinois Press, Champaign.

Bense, J.A. (editor)
1985 Hawkshaw: Prehistory and History in an Urban Neighborhood in Pensacola, Florida. *Reports of Investigations*, No. 7. Office of Cultural and Archaeological Research, University of West Florida, Pensacola.

Breternitz, D.A., C.K. Robinson, and G.T. Gross
1986 *Dolores Archaeological Program: Final Synthetic Report.* U.S. Department of the Interior, Bureau of Reclamation, Engineering and Research Center, Denver.

Brook, G.
1991 Geoarchaeology of the Oconee Reservoir. *Wallace Reservoir Project Contribution* 15. Department of Anthropology, University of Georgia, Athens.

Brose, D.S.
1991 *Yesterday's River; The Archeology of 10,000 Years along the Tennessee-Tombigbee Waterway.* Cleveland Museum of Natural History, Cleveland.

Bush, D.R., and J.E. Thomas
1986a *A Cultural Resource Investigation of selected areas within the Redbird Ranger District, Daniel Boone National Forest, Kentucky.* David Bush, Inc., Cleveland.

1986b *Phase II Assessment Testing od Enoch Fork Shelter (15Pe50), Redbird Ranger District, Daniel Boone National Forest, Kentucky.* David Bush, Inc., Cleveland.

Calabrese, F.A.
1976 Federal Archaeology Legislation and Administration: Intent and Reality, pp. 19-26. *ASCA Proceedings 1976.*

Chapman, J.
1985 *Tellico Archaeology*. University of Tennessee Press, Knoxville.

Collins, M.B. (editor)
1979 Excavations at Four Archaic Sites in the Lower Ohio Valley, Jefferson County, Kentucky. *Occasional Papers in Anthropology*, No. 1. Department of Anthropology, University of Kentucky, Lexington.

Daniel, I.R., Jr., and M. Weisenbaker
1987 *Harney Flats: A Florida Paleo-Indian Site*. Baywood Publishing Co., Inc., Farmingdale, New York.

Faulkner, C.H., and M.C.R. McCollough
1973 Introductory Report of the Normandy Reservoir Salvage Project: Environmental Setting, Typology, and Survey. *Reports of Investigations*, No. 11. Department of Anthropology, University of Tennessee, Knoxville.

Fish, P.R., and D.J. Hally
1983 The Wallace Reservoir Archaeological Project: An Overview. *Early Georgia* 11(1-2):1-19.

Greengrass, M.R.
1993 State Archeology Weeks. *Archeological Assistance Program Technical Brief* 15. U.S. Department of the Interior, National Park Service, Archeological Assistance Division, Washington.

Grumet, R.S. (project coordinator) and M.R. Barnes, S.L. DeVore, H.R. Dunbar, R.S. Grumet, and S.D. Morton (compilers)
1995 Earliest Americans National Historic Landmark Theme Study. Draft 1: Project Description, Status Report, and State Paleo-Indian Archeological Data Summaries. Ms. on file, NPS, Mid-Atlantic Regional Office, Philadelphia.

Ison, C.R.
1988 The Cold Oak Shelter: Providing a Better Understanding of the Terminal Archaic. In *Paleoindian and Archaic Research in Kentucky*, edited by C.C. Hockensmith, D. Pollack, and T. N. Sanders, pp. 205-219. Kentucky Heritage Council, Frankfort.

Keel, B.C., F.P. McManamon, and G.S. Smith (compilers)
1989 *Federal Archeology: The Current Program. Annual Report to Congress on the Federal Archeological Program FY 1985 and FY 1986*. U.S. Department of the Interior, National Park Service, Washington.

Knoll, P.C. (editor)
1990 *Listing of Education in Archeological Programs: The LEAP Clearinghouse. 1987-1989 Summary Report*. U.S. Department of the Interior, National Park Service, Washington.

1993 *Listing of Education in Archeological Programs: The LEAP Clearinghouse. 1990-1992 Summary Report.* U.S. Department of the Interior, National Park Service, Washington.

Knudson, R., and F.P. McManamon
1992 The Secretary's Report to Congress on the Federal Archeology Program. *Federal Archeology Report* 5(2):1,4-10.

Ledbetter, R.J., L.D. O'Steen, and S.A. Kowalewski
1981 Chert of Southern Oconee County, Georgia. *Early Georgia* 9:1-13.

Lipe, W.D., and A.J. Lindsey
1974 Proceedings of the 1974 Cultural Resource Management Conference, Denver, Colorado. *Technical Series* No. 14. Museum of Northern Arizona, Flagstaff.

McManamon, F.P., P.C. Knoll, R. Knudson, G.S. Smith, and R.C. Waldbauer (compilers)
1993 *Federal Archeological Programs and Activities.* U.S. Department of the Interior, National Park Service, Archeological Assistance Division, Departmental Consulting Archeologist, Washington.

Moratto, M.J., J.D. Tordoff, and L.H. Sharp, with contributions by others
1988 Culture Change in the Central Sierra Nevada, 8,000 B.C.-A.D. 1950. *Final Report of the New Melones Archeological Project* Vol. 9. Report to the National Park Service, Washington, D.C. INFOTEC Development, Inc., Sonora, California.

Orr, D.G., and D.V. Campara (editors)
1991 *The Peopling of Minisink. Papers from the 1989 Delaware Water Gap Symposium.* National Park Service, Mid-Atlantic Region, Philadelphia.

O'Steen, L.D., R.J. Ledbetter, D.T. Elliott, and W.W. Barker
1986 Paleoindian Sites of the Inner Piedmont of Georgia: Observations of Settlement in the Oconee Watershed. *Early Georgia* 1:13-63.

Smith, G.S., and J.E. Ehrenhard (editors)
1991 *Protecting the Past.* CRC Press, Boca Raton, Florida.

Society for American Archaeology (SAA)
1991 *Save the Past for the Future: Action Plan for the '90s.* Society for American Archaeology, Washington.

Ward M., J. Burr, and J. Ahler
1989 *The Mouse Raid.* University of North Dakota Press, Grand Forks.

List of Contributors

Judith A. Bense is the Director, Archaeology Institute, and Associate Professor of Anthropology, University of West Florida, Pensacola.

Robson Bonnichsen is the Director, Center for the Study of the First Americans, and Associate Professor of Anthropology, Oregon State University, Corvallis.

F.A. Calabrese is the Chief, Midwest Archeological Center, National Park Service, U.S. Department of the Interior, Lincoln, Nebraska, and an Adjunct Professor of Anthropology, University of Nebraska, Lincoln.

Heather Devine is an independent cultural heritage consultant and former Education Officer of the Archaeological Survey of Alberta, Provincial Museum of Alberta, Edmonton.

Tom D. Dillehay is a Professor of Anthropology, University of Kentucky, Lexington, and the Departamento de Antropologia, Universidad de Chile, Valdivia.

John G. Douglas is a Senior Archeologist, Division of Cultural Resources, Bureau of Land Management, U.S. Department of the Interior, Washington.

John M. Fowler is the Senior Counsel, Advisory Council on Historic Preservation, Washington.

George C. Frison is a Professor of Anthropology, University of Wyoming, Laramie.

Roy A. Gallant is Director/Lecturer of the Southworth Planetarium and Adjunct Professor of English, University of Southern Maine, Portland.

Leslie Starr Hart is Chief, Office of Professional and Employee Development, Denver Service Center, National Park Service, U.S. Department of the Interior, Denver, and at the time of the symposium was Chief, Division of Cultural Resources, Alaska Regional Office, National Park Service, U.S. Department of the Interior, Anchorage.

Fumiko Ikawa-Smith is a Professor of Anthropology, McGill University, Montreal.

Bennie C. Keel is the Southeast Regional Archeologist, Southeast Archeological Center, National Park Service, U.S. Department of the Interior, Tallahassee, and Adjunct Professor of Anthropology,

Florida State University, Tallahassee. At the time of the symposium he was National Park Service Assistant Director-Archeology and the U.S. Department of the Interior Departmental Consulting Archeologist.

Ruthann Knudson is an Archeologist, Archeological Assistance Division and Office of the Departmental Consulting Archeologist, National Park Service, U.S. Department of the Interior, Washington; Research Associate, California Academy of Sciences, San Francisco; and principal of her own small woman-owned firm, Knudson Associates, Alexandria, Virginia.

Dennis C. Le Master is the Head, Department of Forestry and Natural Resources, Purdue University, West Lafayette, Indiana.

Francis P. McManamon is the U.S. Department of the Interior Departmental Consulting Archeologist and Chief, Archeological Assistance Division, National Park Service, U.S. Department of the Interior, Washington.

Martin P.R. Magne is currently Chief of Archaeological Services, Parks Canada, Alberta Region, Calgary, and at the time of the symposium was the Head, Archaeological Survey of Alberta, Alberta Provincial Museum, Edmonton.

Charles R. McGimsey III, is now Director Emeritus, Arkansas Archeological Survey, and Professor Emeritus of Anthropology, University of Arkansas, Fayetteville.

Dennis Stanford is a Curator of Anthropology, Director of the Paleoindian Program, and Chair, Department of Anthropology, National Museum of Natural History, Smithsonian Institution, Washington.

D. Gentry Steele is a Professor of Anthropology, Texas A&M University, College Station.

Allan R. Taylor is a specialist in the linguistics of North American Indians and is a Professor of Linguistics, University of Colorado, Boulder.

John Tomenchuk is a Research Associate, Royal Ontario Museum, Toronto.

Patty Jo Watson is a Distinguished University Professor of Anthropology, Washington University, St. Louis, Missouri.

Stephen Williams is Emeritus Professor and the Honorary Curator of North American Archaeology, Peabody Museum of Archaeology and Ethnology, Harvard University, Cambridge, Massachusetts, and was Peabody Professor and Curator at the time of the symposium.

Index

Abandoned Shipwreck Act of 1987, 81, 101-102

Advisory Council on Historic Preservation, 78, 79, 84, 101, 199

Alberta, 93, 102, 130; Historical Resources Act of, 98; Archaeological Survey of, 98-99; Calgary, 100, 128-129, 137; Environment Conservation Authority of, 98, 104

American Indian Religious Freedom Act, 80

Antiquities Act of 1906, 13, 51, 55, 58, 176, 188

Archaeological and Shipwreck Information System, 39

Archaeological Resource Protection Act, 5, 13, 51, 53, 55, 79, 101, 119, 122, 158, 176-179

archaeological resources: *in situ* conservation of, 19, 31, 51, 53, 54, 58, 62-63, 96; inventory of, 5-6, 54-55, 57, 79-80, 89, 120-121, 176, 192-194; looting of, 49, 51, 73, 80, 89, 140-141, 199; management of, 3-6, 19, 49-50, 55-57, 99, 173-182, 185, 192, 197-198 (*see also* management); quantities, 5-6, 121; submerged, 17, 39, 81, 88, 97; trafficking, 49, 74, 96, 97; value of, 12, 18, 19, 51, 185

archaeologists, amateur/avocational, vii, 57, 59, 100, 119, 177, 200, 202

Archeological and Historic Preservation Act of 1974, 13, 51, 54, 78, 124, 158, 191

Arctic Research and Policy Act of 1984, 3-4

artifacts, 89, 100; classification of, 40; core and flake tool patterns, 34; curation of, 21, 100, 121, 123-124, 163-164; fishtail point complex, 34; projectile point styles, 33-34; Upper Paleolithic technology, 36-37

Asia, 4, 30-32, 35, 37, 39, 41, 46-48, 53, 87-90, 115, 190

Auel, Jean, 62, 64

Australia, 47-48, 73

Automatic Manager of Archeological Site Data in Arkansas, 39

bioanthropology. *See* research

Bureau of Indian Affairs, 174

Bureau of Land Management, 52, 121, 124, 134, 173-175, 177, 178, 187, 189

Bureau of Reclamation, 121, 124, 159, 174, 193, 195

California, 15, 175, 195

Canada, 49, 50, 52, 55, 57, 74, 75, 76, 84-85, 93-105, 130-131, 163 (*see also* Alberta): Archaeological Survey of, Rescue Archaeology Program, 95; Canadian Antiquities Act (suggested), 95-96; Canadian Archaeological Association, 95-98, 102, 104, 200; Departments of Canadian Heritage, 102, Communications, 93, 96-98, 102-104, Environment, 96; Indian and Northern Affairs, 96-97, 104, Transport, 96; Canadian Environmental Assessment Act of 1994, 52, 95; Canadian Federal Heritage Building Review Office, 84; Canadian Museum of Civilization, 94, 95, 103; Canadian Parks Service, 94, 95, 188; Department of Indian and Northern Affairs Development Act (Indian Act), 84, 94

Center for the Study of the First Americans, ix-x, 2, 40, 140, 142, 144

Central America, 4, 48, 49, 87-90, 197

Chile, 90, 164

Chippendale, Christopher, 11, 22

Cleere, Henry, 10, 22, 50, 66

climatic change. *See* paleoenvironment; research.

Clovis, 33, 37, 48, 115, 162, 163

compliance archaeology. *See* archaeological resources, management

Cultural Property Export and Import Act, 96, 102

cultural resources, 10, 17, 56, 88-89, 121, 178, 181

Defense Technical Information Service. *See* U.S. Department of Defense.

Departmental Consulting Archeologist. *See* U.S. Department of the Interior.